Disney's
BIG
BAD
BOOK
· OF ·
PUZZLERS

DEVIOUSLY DIFFICULT GAMES AND BRAINTEASERS FEATURING FAVORITE DISNEY VILLAINS

KAREN C. ANDERSON

Disney
PRESS

NEW YORK

Illustrated by Scott Tilley, Judie Clarke,
Leticia Lichtwardt, Laura Nichols, Lureline Kohler,
Thomas S. Phong, and Russell Schroeder

Printed in the United States of America.

First Edition
1 3 5 7 9 10 8 6 4 2

Library of Congress Catalog Card Number: 94-74820
ISBN: 0-7868-4032-3

Cruella De Vil has a long list of favorite words. Seventeen of them are hidden in the word-search grid below. Look for the words in straight lines reading across, back, up, down, and diagonally.

ABOMINABLE
BLACKHEARTED
DETESTABLE
DIABOLICAL
FIENDISH
HATEFUL
HEINOUS
INFAMOUS
INFERNAL
LOATHSOME
MALIGNANT
NEFARIOUS
ROTTEN
SINISTER
VICIOUS
VILLAINOUS
WRETCHED

```
V I N F E R N A L H E F L
B I H E I N O U S L A O U
W L L V N E G E B L A T R
R M A L I G N A N T R E E
E L C C A L N D H I L B T
T U I L K I L S I B O S S
C F L B M H O A A S U T I
H E O O C M E T I O H I N
E T B A E A S A M N S N I
D A A T N E F A R I O U S
I H I H T L F C N T I U O
A L D E O N R O T T E N S
B O D V I C I O U S M D T
```

7

Answers on
page 149

Hey! Rafiki has headphones on! There are at least 10 other mistakes in this scene based on *The Lion King*. How many can you find?

Answers on page 149

When Jafar becomes a genie, he sends Aladdin out of town in a sandstorm. Can you unscramble all the jumbled words below to form the names of 14 other types of bad weather and natural disasters?

1. ARIN _____
2. LIHA _____
3. RIEF _____
4. OLDFO _____
5. TELSE _____
6. CAVLOON _____
7. SNOMOON _____
8. HOTGURD _____
9. REDHUNT _____
10. DOORNAT _____
11. RIZZBALD _____
12. MIDDLEUS _____
13. URCHINEAR _____
14. QUEAKHEART _____

Answers on
page 149

The wily witch is whisking up a potion with which to poison Snow White. Many of the items in her workshop begin with the letter W. If you can find 10 of them, that's wonderful!

10

11

Answers on
page 149

Aim to Win

Gaston is playing darts. In order to win, he has to score 69 points with five darts, with no two darts landing on the same number. How can he win?

50
25
20
10
5
3
2
1

12

Answers on
page 149

Here are three pictures of Kaa, that sneaky snake from *The Jungle Book*. Can you tell which of the three positions will make a knot in his body if you pulled his head and tail?

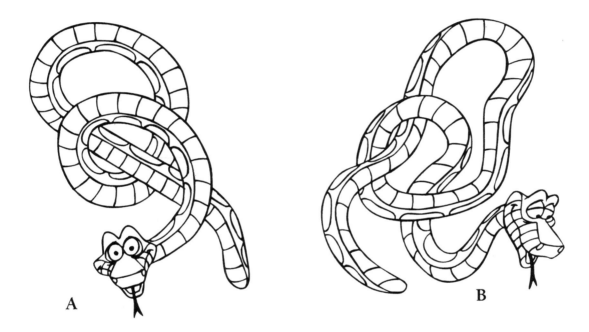

A

B

C

13

Answers on page 150

Draw a straight line from the circle next to the villain on the left to the circle by the matching sidekick on the right. Then take the letters crossed by the lines and write them in the spaces below, matching the number beside each villain's name to the ones below the spaces. If you've drawn the links correctly, the letters will spell a bonus word.

Cruella De Vil ①   M   ○ Iago

                  R

Jafar ②   C   ○ LeFou

                  O

Gaston ③   T   ○ Smee

                  A

                  S

Ursula ④   L   ○ Jasper and Horace

                  V

Scar ⑤   U   ○ The Raven

                  E

Captain Hook ⑥   B   ○ Flotsam and Jetsam

                  I

Maleficent ⑦   N   ○ Banzai, Shenzi, and Ed

14

___ ___ ___ ___ ___ ___ ___
1   2   3   4   5   6   7

There are 10 differences between these two scenes based on *The Little Mermaid*. Can you spot them all?

Answers on page 150

Deep Trouble

Monstro the giant whale is after Pinocchio and Geppetto! Can you find a path through this watery maze and help them escape to the safety of the rocks?

finish

start

16

Answers on page 150

Cinderella's cruel stepmother, Lady Tremaine, has a stately name. That is, the state of *MAINE* appears in her name. Can you find the states hidden in the sentences below? You can ignore any punctuation, but the letters of each state appear in order.

1. Did you see the *Queen Mary* land?
2. The Swiss miss is sipping hot cocoa.
3. Johnny, it is okay to color a donkey green.
4. Be sure to correctly match cities to states; Denver, Montana, is incorrect.
5. When the tide comes in, is the shore gone?
6. Radio waves can travel farther at night.
7. I want to redecorate in salmon, tan, and olive.
8. Are you doing the washing tonight or tomorrow?
9. Oh! I only bought enough popcorn for two.
10. Anita—who hid a horse in Harold's house?

17

Answers on
page 151

Coin Collectors

Ratcliffe has to gather a lot of money to pay for his voyage to Virginia but his servant, Wiggins, can carry only two bags of coins. Which two bags should Ratcliffe have Wiggins carry to bring the most money? How much will they have?

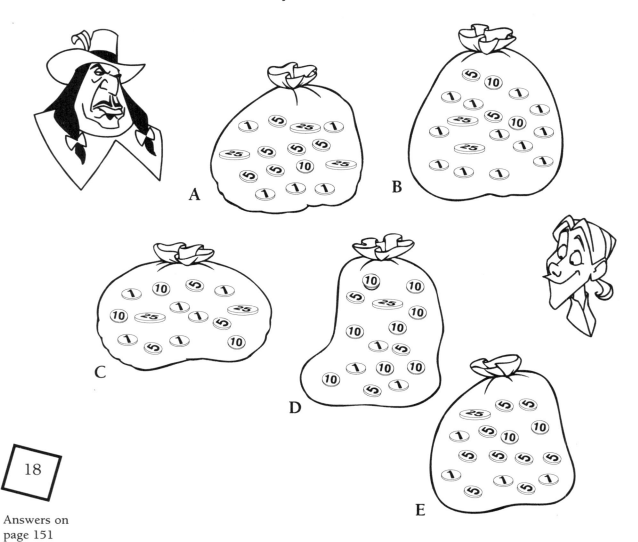

A

B

C

D

E

Answers on
page 151

When you finish this puzzle, you'll have drawn a couple of nasty characters from a Disney film. To find out who they are, draw what you see in box 2C into the square in row 2 and column C in the blank grid. Do the same with each square until all 20 boxes are filled in.

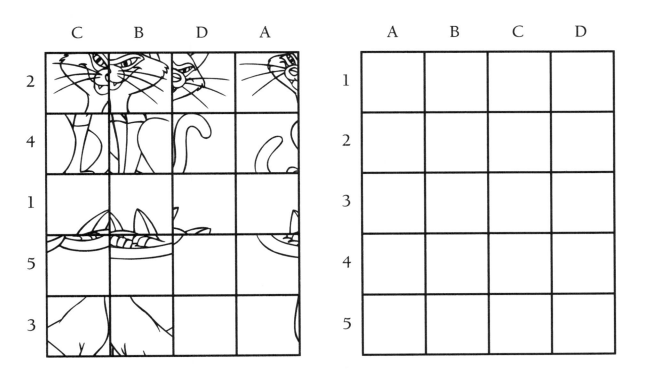

19

Answers on
page 151

Of the pack of hyenas circling Simba and Nala,
only two are exactly alike. Can you find them?

A

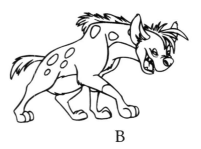

B

C

D

Answers on
page 151

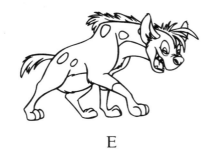

E

F

Maleficent is ordering her goons to find Princess Aurora. Which of the boxes at the bottom of the page is taken exactly from the scene?

A   B   C   D

Answers on page 151

MIX

The six villains here all want to get home.
However, villains usually try to avoid each other,
so they don't want to use any of the same paths or

Answers on
page 152

even cross any of the others' paths. Can you draw lines to connect each villain to his or her home?

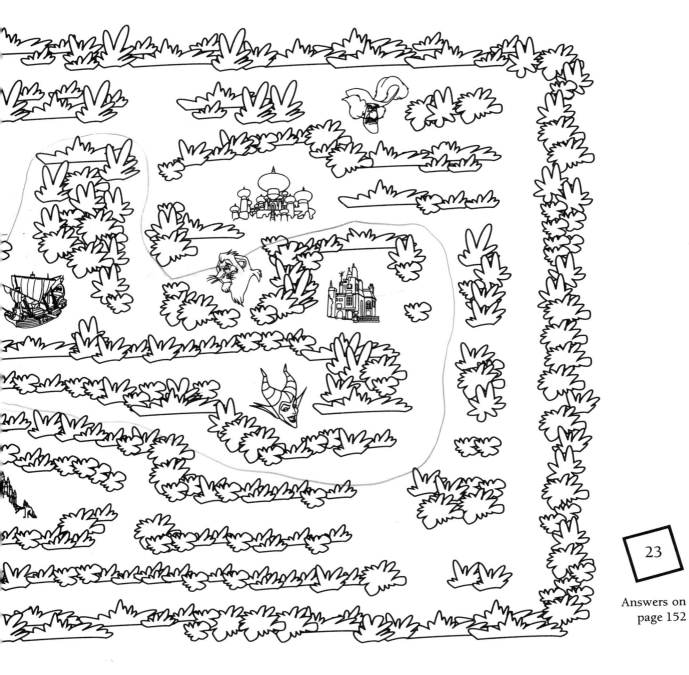

Below is a treasure map that Captain Hook found. If you follow the directions carefully, you will find out where the prize is buried.

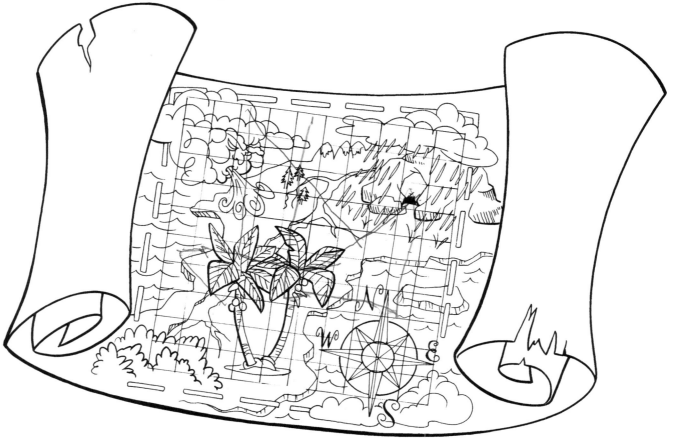

1. Start at the cave entrance and go four squares southwest.
2. Travel four squares west.
3. Go two squares southeast.
4. March eight squares north.
5. Go four squares southeast.
6. End at the treasure, two squares northeast.

Answers on
page 152

Ten Tons

Gaston's name contains the word *TON*. So do the 10 words defined below. Can you fill in all the blanks?

1. Taste-bud location _____
2. Another word for rock _____
3. This evening _____
4. A majorette twirls one _____
5. Low, fold-up bed _____
6. Container for milk _____
7. Shirt fastener _____
8. Shirt material _____
9. Capital of the United States _____
10. "Grand" mountains in Wyoming _____

25

Answers on
page 153

Image Problems

In *The Little Mermaid,* Ursula poses as a pretty maiden and uses Ariel's voice to woo Prince Eric. But her mirror reflection still shows her true self. In the scene below, there are lots of other things that aren't reflected correctly in the mirror. Can you find at least ten?

26

Answers on page 153

How well do you remember details? In this scene, Ratcliffe is getting his men ready for battle. Study this picture for up to three minutes, then turn the page to test your memory.

27

Answers on page 153

The eight questions below refer to the scene based on *Pocahontas* on page 27. If you can answer five or more correctly, you've got a battle-worthy memory.

1. Is Ratcliffe holding a weapon?
2. Where is Percy the dog?
3. What is on the ground in the lower-left-hand corner of the scene?
4. Which one of these things is not in the scene?

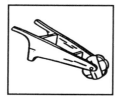   

5. How many men are in the scene?
6. What is on Wiggins's front pocket?
7. What can be seen inside the tent?
8. What is being built at the settlement?

Answers on page 153

The Queen of Hearts said she won't cut off Alice's head if Alice can find the stack of blocks that contains exactly 38 cubes. Assuming all the structures are solid behind the parts you can see, which stack should Alice choose?

Answers on page 153

These six swordsmen from the palace all share something besides their loyalty to Jafar. Can you spot the one thing they all have in common?

Dark Spot

In *Sleeping Beauty,* Maleficent and her goons live in a dark and creepy place. To find out where, answer the four clues below. Then write each letter in the matching numbered box at the bottom of the page to spell out the name of Maleficent's home. (Some numbers appear more than once in the top section.)

1. Clothing worn by an army officer or a postal worker

    ___ ___ ___ ___ ___ ___ ___
    12   9   16   1   11   3   10

2. Thickly treed area

    ___ ___ ___ ___ ___ ___
     1   11   3   8   15   14

3. Marching instrumental group

    ___ ___ ___ ___
     4   15   13   6

4. Rectangular game piece with two sets of zero to six dots

    ___ ___ ___ ___ ___ ___
     7   11   10   5   17   2

    ___ ___ ___ ___ ___ ___ ___ ___ ___
     1   2   3   4   5   6   7   8   9

    ___ ___ ___ ___ ___ ___ ___ ___ ___
    10   11   12   13   14   15   16   17   18

31

Answers on page 154

Through the Cracks

The last time the evil Queen from *Snow White* asked the Magic Mirror a question, the glass cracked. If you color in every piece of the cracked mirror that has exactly four sides, you'll discover a hidden picture.

32

Answers on page 154

Word Hound

How many words of four or more letters can you spell using only the letters in *DOGCATCHER*? You may use a letter more than once only if it appears in *DOGCATCHER* more than once (like *C*). We rounded up 70 words; if you can find 60 or more, you're a real word hound!

DOGCATCHER

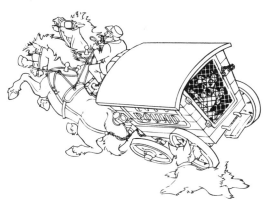

Catch, read, _____

_____

_____

_____

_____

_____

_____

_____

_____

_____

_____

33

Answers on page 154

Canine Rebuses

The answers to the rebuses below will reveal four types of canines. Can you solve the picture puzzles and name all of them?

To solve a rebus, add and subtract the letters of the words that are illustrated as shown.

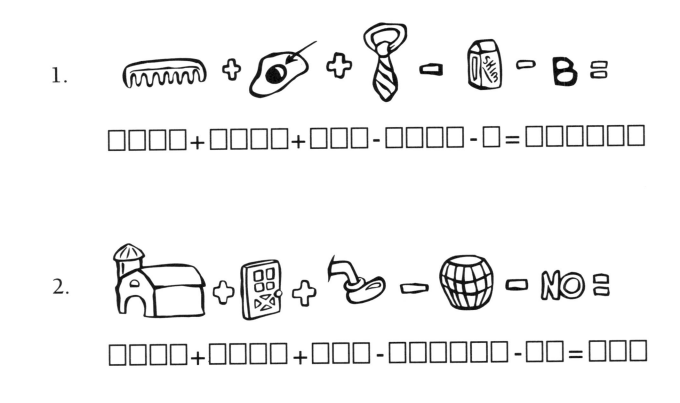

3.

□□□□□ + □□□ + □□□□ - □□□□ - □□□□ = □□□□

4.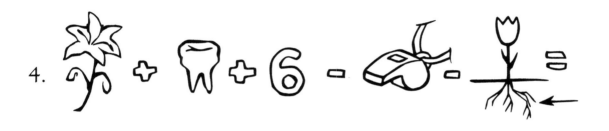

□□□□□□ + □□□□□ + □□□ - □□□□□□□□

-□□□□ = □□□

Each of the crosswords on these two pages is made up of a set of related words. We've given you the category and some of the letters as a guide. Can you complete the grids?

1. HATS
The evil Queen has filled in *CROWN*. Can you figure out the rest of the words?

2. HOMES
Maleficent wrote in her *CASTLE*. What are the other dwellings?

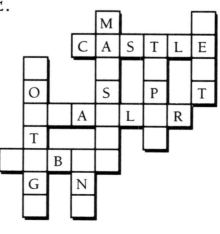

Answers on page 155

3. GEMS
Although Ratcliffe loves gold best, he would take a *DIAMOND* any day.
What other gemstones are in this grid?

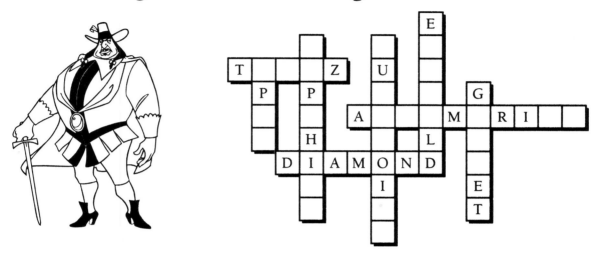

4. BODIES OF WATER
Ursula likes the *OCEAN* and has written it in. Can you fill in the other bodies of water?

37

Answers on page 155

Fishing Lines

The sea can be a dangerous place. Can you draw three straight lines to separate Ariel, Flounder, and Sebastian from the deadly sharks and eels?

38

Answers on
page 155

Kingdom Come

Alphabetize this list of animals and characters from *The Lion King* and write them in the squares below. Then read down the shaded column to find out Scar's reply to Simba's question: "When I'm king, what will that make you?"

MUFASA
RHINOCEROS
CHAMELEON
ZEBRA
PUMBAA
HIPPOPOTAMUS
SCAR
MEERKAT
BANZAI
WILDEBEEST
MONKEY
LION KING
HYENA

39

Answers on
page 155

Pinocchio and Lampwick are playing billiards on Pleasure Island. Can you figure out which of the shots pictured below will send a ball into a hole, assuming only one cue ball is on the table at a time? If Pinocchio is shooting at solids and Lampwick at stripes, who will sink more balls?

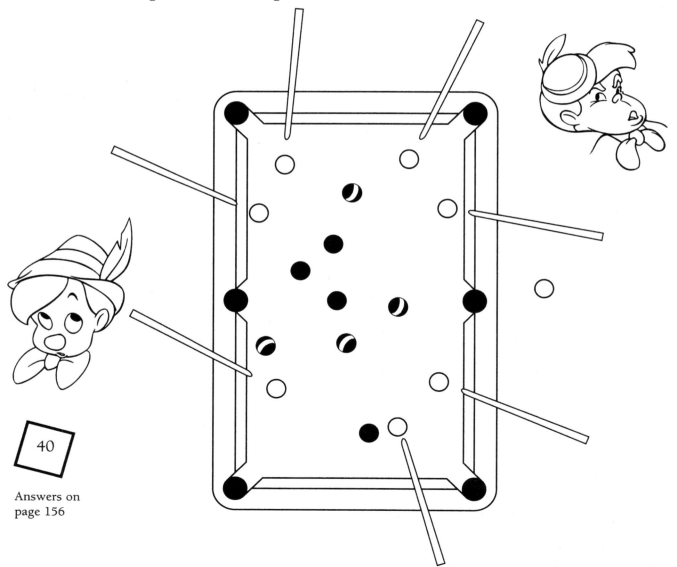

When Aladdin is in the dungeon, Jafar disguises himself as an old man and tells Aladdin his version of the golden rule. To find out what it is, answer the six clues below. Then write each letter in the matching numbered box at the bottom of the page to spell out Jafar's golden rule.

1. Stubborn pack animal; the offspring of a donkey and a horse

___ ___ ___ ___
18 27 16 13

2. Mitten with fingers

___ ___ ___ ___ ___
14 28 3   5   25

3. Dentures replace them

___ ___ ___ ___ ___
11 6   21 23 2

4. Great White sea creature

___ ___ ___ ___ ___
22 12 9   7   20

5. Alternative to a bath

___ ___ ___ ___ ___ ___
10 24 15 1   29 26

6. Relief from the sun, as provided by trees

___ ___ ___ ___ ___
30 8   19 17 4

"___ ___ ___ ___ ___ ___ ___   ___ ___ ___
  1   2   3   4   5   6   7   8   9   10

___ ___ ___   ___ ___ ___ ___
11 12 13   14 15 16 17

___ ___ ___ ___ ___   ___ ___ ___
18 19 20 21 22   23 24 25

___ ___ ___ ___ ___."
26 27 28 29 30

41

Answers on page 156

S Curves

A sea squall is tossing Ratcliffe's ship, the *Susan Constant*. Lots of items that begin with the letter *S* are slipping and sliding around. Can you spot at least 25 things that begin with *S* in this stormy scene?

42

Answers on page 156

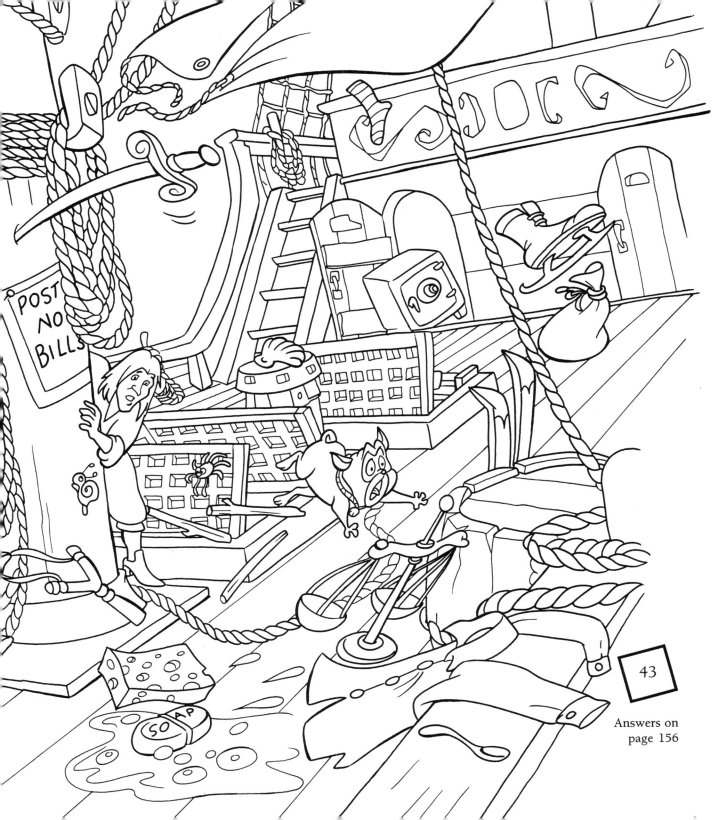

POST NO BILLS

SOAP

43

Answers on page 156

Body Check

Kaa has something hidden in his coils. To find out what it is, color in all the segments that contain exactly two dots.

44

Answers on
page 157

Cruella De Vil is searching for the Dalmatian puppies in the barnyard. The animals have each given her a clue about which of them is hiding the puppies. They're all telling the truth, but Cruella still can't figure out the answer. Can you?

I am smarter than the cat.

I am smarter than the oldest animal but not as smart as the youngest animal.

I also am smarter than the oldest animal but not as smart as the youngest animal.

The puppies are hiding with the oldest animal.

45

Answers on page 157

How many words of four or more letters can you spell using only the letters in *PRINCE JOHN*? You may use a letter more than once only if it appears in *PRINCE JOHN* more than once (like *N*). If you find 35 or more, you are a king of words.

Chin, chip, _____

_____

_____

_____

_____

_____

_____

Answers on page 157

Gaston is looking at tracks in the snow to try to track down the Beast. Can you determine the order in which the following passed by?

WOLF   BEAST
BELLE   HORSE AND WAGON
MAURICE   BIRD

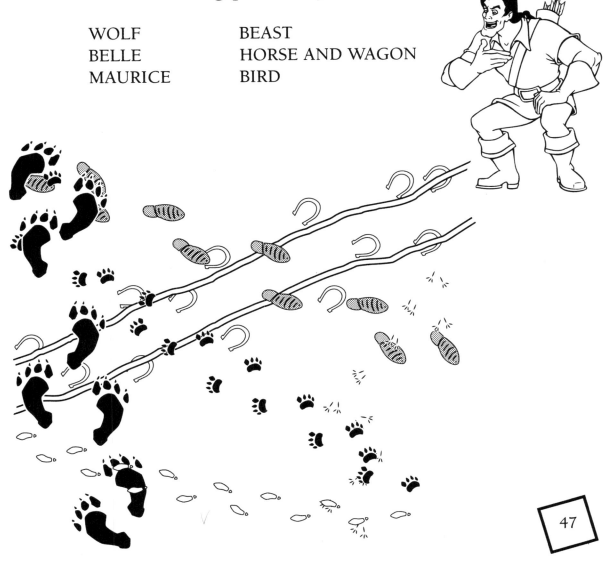

Answers on
page 157

These six rough-looking fellows are all pirates on Captain Hook's ship. Besides that, can you spot one thing that they all have in common?

Answers on
page 157

Lady Tremaine and her obnoxious daughters are practicing their dance steps for the king's ball. Fifteen dances are hidden in the grid below. Can you find them? They are spelled out in straight lines reading across, back, up, down, and diagonally.

BELLY DANCE
BOLERO
BUNNY HOP
CAKEWALK
CAN-CAN
CHARLESTON
FOX-TROT
HOKEYPOKEY
HUSTLE
LIMBO
POLKA
TANGO
TWIST
TWO-STEP
WALTZ

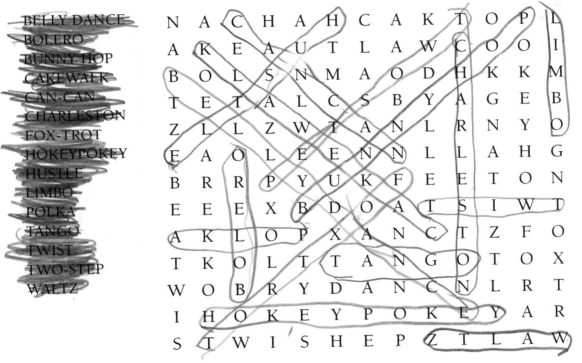

```
N A C H A H C A K T O P L
A K E A U T L A W C O O I
B O L S N M A O D H K K M
T E T A L C S B Y A G E B
Z L L Z W T A N L R N Y O
E A O L E E N N L L A H G
B R R P Y U K F E E T O N
E E E X B D O A T S I W T
A K L O P X A N C T Z F O
T K O L T T A N G O T O X
W O B R Y D A N C N L R T
I H O K E Y P O K E Y A R
S T W I S H E P Z T L A W
```

49

Answers on page 158

Skinny and his friends are taunting Dumbo about his big ears. There are 10 differences between the top and bottom pictures. Can you spot them all?

Answers on
page 158

Banzai's name contains the word *BAN*. So do the 10 words defined below. Can you identify all the words?

1. Yellow fruit _____
2. Not in the city _____
3. Wrap for a wound _____
4. Handrail by the stairway _____
5. Place to keep coins _____
6. Stringed instrument _____
7. Person from Havana _____
8. Feast _____
9. Head wrap worn by Muslims _____
10. Crook; thief _____

Answers on
page 158

Can you match the villains (1 to 8) to their hair (*A* to *H*) on the opposite page?

1. CAPTAIN HOOK A

2. CRUELLA DE VIL E

3. GASTON G

4. LADY TREMAINE D

5. QUEEN OF HEARTS B

6. SCAR C

7. URSULA H

8. WITCH E

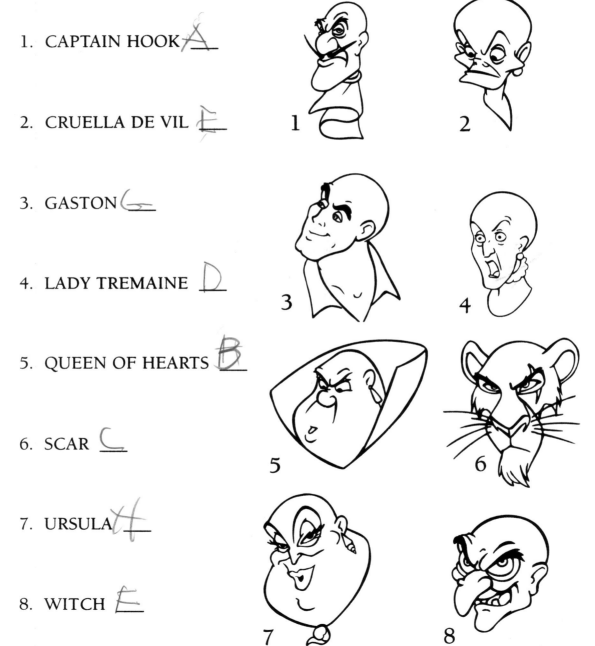

52

Answers on page 158

A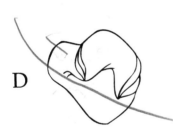

B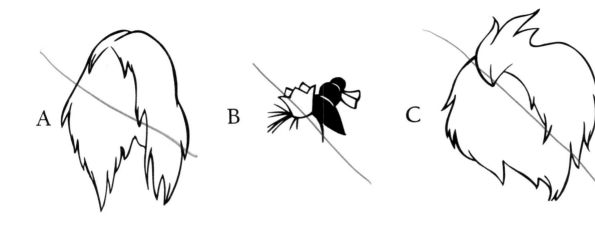

C

D

E

F

G

H

Answers on page 158

Jafar wants to catch Aladdin, the street rat, stealing food. However, Aladdin has to resort to stealing food on only one day every month. Use the clues below to figure out which day of the month Jafar should try to catch Aladdin.

1. Aladdin eats with his neighbors on weekends.

2. For two days on and then one day off, starting on the first and continuing throughout the month, Aladdin works at a bakery. On the days he works he gets free food.

3. Every Monday, Wednesday, and Friday, Aladdin buys food with money he and Abu earn by performing in the streets.

4. On even-numbered days of the month, a local food vendor gives Aladdin and Abu the food he doesn't sell for that day.

SUN	MON	TUES	WEDS	THURS	FRI	SAT
1	2	3	4	5	6	7
8	9	10	11	12	13	14
15	16	17	18	19	20	21
22	23	24	25	26	27	28
29	30					

Answers on
page 158

Take-Outs II

As Snow White runs through the forest at night, the trees and logs look like terrifying monsters. Which of the boxes at the bottom of the page is taken exactly from the scene?

A   B   C   D

55

Answers on page 158

Hot Air

Maleficent has transformed herself into a dragon and is breathing fire. The flames are forming a picture. Connect the dots in order from 1 to 49 to find out what it is.

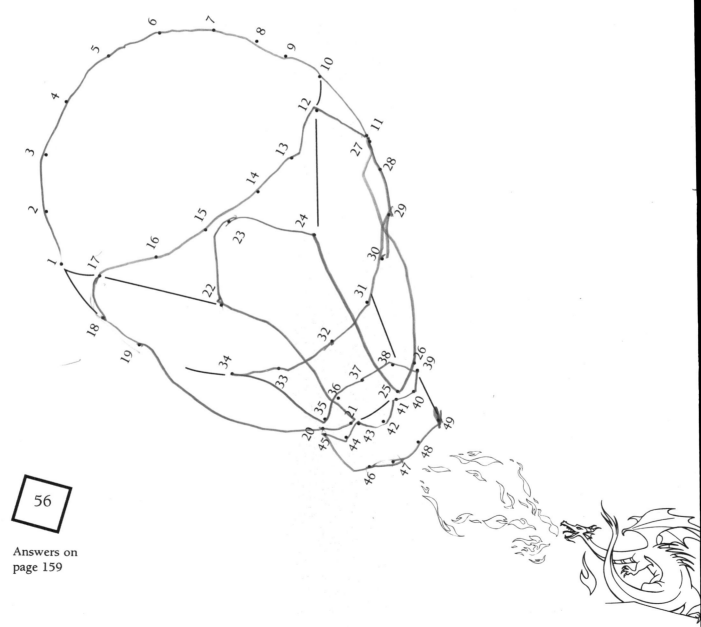

56

Answers on page 159

Can you insert mathematical symbols (+, −, x, ÷) into the sets of twos below to make each equation match its answer? One equation is finished to start you off. (There may be more than one answer for some of the equations.)

Example: $0 = 2 - 2 + 2 - 2$

1 = 2   2   2   2
2 = 2   2   2   2
3 = 2   2   2   2
4 = 2   2   2   2
5 = 2   2   2   2
6 = 2   2   2   2
8 = 2   2   2   2

Answers on
page 159

Silence!

Governor John Ratcliffe has collected a list of words containing silent letters. His name has two—the *H* in his first name and the *E* in his last name are both silent. How many of the words defined below can you name? The silent letters are given on the left as clues.

B   1. Hair detangler   _____

C   2. Biology or chemistry   _____

D   3. Middle day of the school week   _____

G   4. Four times two   _____

H   5. Haunting figure   _____

K   6. Way to connect two strings   _____

L   7. Name of a fish, or a shade of pink _____

N   8. Another word for pillar   _____

P   9. Small, red, seedy berry   _____

T   10. Art form in which you point your
           toes and wear a tutu   _____

W   11. Which person?   _____

Answers on
page 159

There are several dogs in this scene based on *Lady and the Tramp,* but you might not see them at first glance because they're hiding from the dogcatcher. Can you find at least six dogs?

59

Answers on page 160

Symbol Crash

Gaston is playing a game with his friends at the tavern. Can you help him finish? The empty boxes must be filled in with the **names of five animals** according to these rules:

- No animal may **appear** twice in any row or column.
- No animal may **appear** twice in any corner-to-corner diagonal row.
- The animals that **are** already placed on the board may not be moved.

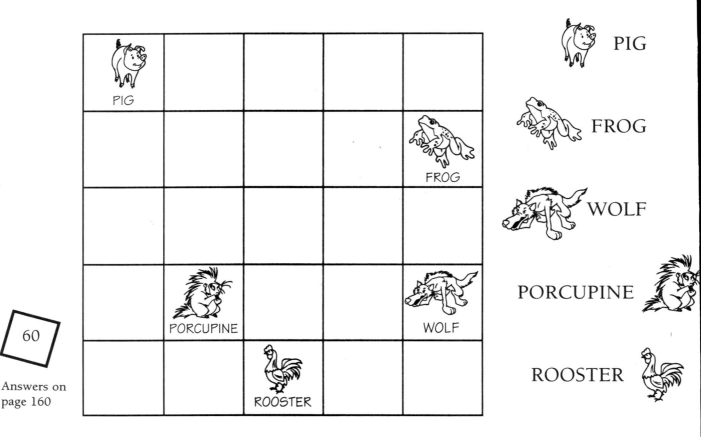

Answers on page 160

Draw a straight line from the circle next to the poison apple on the left to the circle by the matching poison apple on the right. Then take the letters crossed by the lines and write them in the spaces below, matching the numbers on the left with the ones below the spaces. If you've drawn the links correctly, the letters will spell a bonus word.

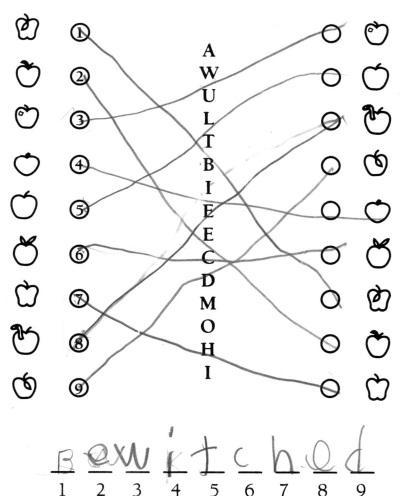

A
W
U
L
T
B
I
E
E
C
D
M
O
H
I

B e w i t c h e d

1 2 3 4 5 6 7 8 9

61

Answers on page 160

62

Answers on
page 160

There's something strange going on here! Can you find at least 10 things wrong in this scene based on *The Jungle Book*?

Answers on page 160

Can you figure out the hidden names of the three Disney villains below? Fill in the blanks so that a three-letter word reads down each column. There may be more than one three-letter word that will work for some, but only the right ones will spell out the villains' names!

EXAMPLE: E   L   O   I   D   B   A   A
          <u>V</u>   <u>I</u>   <u>L</u>   <u>L</u>   <u>A</u>   <u>I</u>   <u>N</u>   <u>S</u>
          E   E   D   L   Y   D   D   H

1. G   P   A   O   F   M
    —   —   —   —   —   —
    M   O   K   T   Y   D

2. A   Z   U   S   H   I
    —   —   —   —   —   —
    E   P   E   Y   G   N

3. I   J   A   T   O   D   I   K   E   A
    —   —   —   —   —   —   —   —   —   —
    P   M   L   E   F   M   E   Y   D   E

64

Answers on
page 161

Stromboli has just hired a new puppet for his show. Connect the dots in order from 1 to 58 to see what the puppet looks like.

65

Answers on page 161

Bambi's mother can sense that man is in the forest. By studying the scene below, can you see where he is?

Answers on
page 161

Like JasMINe, all the words defined below contain the letters *MIN*. Can you guess them all?

1. Popular flavor for gum or chocolate _____
2. Sixty seconds _____
3. Black-and-white game piece _____
4. _____ and minerals _____
5. Tall, pink bird _____
6. U.S. inventor and statesman _____ Franklin
7. Bendable light silver metal used for foil _____
8. Very small _____
9. St. Paul's state _____
10. Thanksgiving raisin-and-nut pie _____

67

Answers on page 162

Ratcliffe has noticed that each of these six settlers is different from all the others in at least one way. Can you pinpoint the reason why each character stands alone? (In some cases, your answers may not be the same as ours.)

Answers on
page 162

Cinderella's spiteful stepmother has broken the clock at the palace so that Cinderella won't be able to tell when it's midnight. Can you put the pieces of the clock back together and figure out what time it is?

69

Answers on page 162

Vanishing Valuables

Answers on
page 162

Ursula the Sea Witch has taken Ariel's voice and hidden it in her sea cave. There are at least 20 other things here that begin with V. If you can find at least 15, consider yourself victorious.

71

Answers on page 162

The letters in *SCAR* can be rearranged to make the word *CARS*. *SCAR* and *CARS* are anagrams of each other. In the same way, the letters in the words defined on the left below can be rearranged to spell the names of the things pictured on the right. How many anagrams can you name?

1. They are defined in the dictionary

— — — — —   — — — — —

2. Rodents bigger than mice

— — — —   — — — —

3. Slink around

— — — — —   — — — — —

4. Something teachers hate

— — —   — — —

5. Edge of the ocean

— — — — —   — — — — —

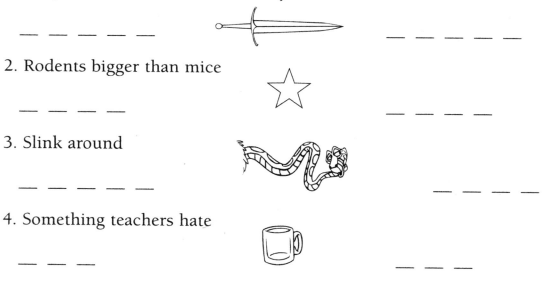

72

Answers on page 162

Captain Hook is making Wendy walk the plank. As she walks out over the water, she starts seeing shapes in the waves. Color in every shape that has exactly two bubbles in it to reveal a picture.

73

Answers on page 163

When you finish this puzzle, you'll have drawn a certain short-tempered character from a Disney film. To find out who it is, draw what you see in box 3B into the square in row 3 and column B in the blank grid. Do the same with each square until all 20 boxes are filled in.

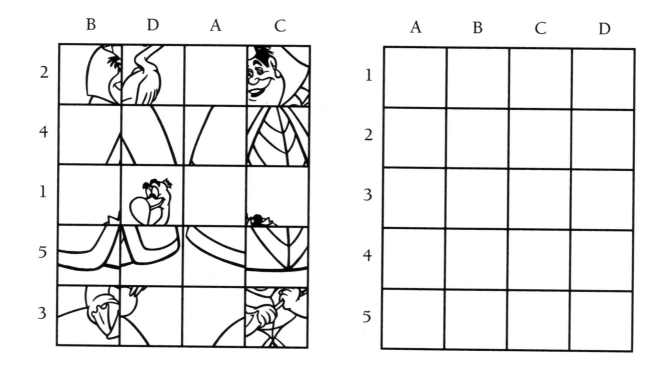

Answers on
page 163

Can you find the path through the forest that will lead Gaston to the Beast? Be sure to avoid the wolves!

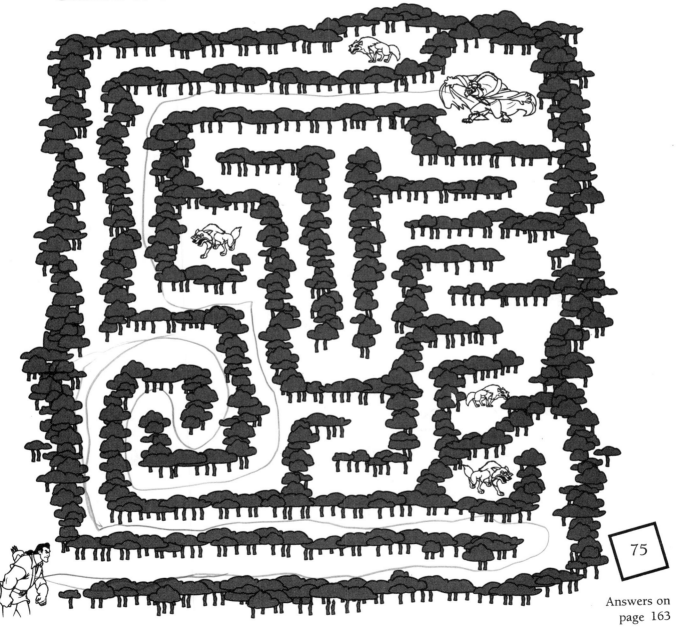

75

Answers on page 163

Cruella De Vil has shown up at Roger and Anita's house. But since she's arrived everything has gone topsy-turvy. For instance, the colors of the piano keys are backward. There are at least nine other mistakes in this scene—can you find them all?

76

Answers on page 163

77

Answers on
page 163

In this game, you will change the word *RAVEN* into another word, one letter at a time. Answer each definition with a word that is one letter different from the word before it. The last word will tell you what happened to Maleficent's raven at the end of *Sleeping Beauty*.

RAVEN

1. Goes nuts over   _____
2. Gives a score to   _____
3. Traditional rituals   _____
4. What dough does   _____
5. Dangers   _____
6. Ice-skating arenas   _____
7. Bands for fingers   _____
8. Performs in a choir   _____
9. Burn like hair in a candle _____
10. A persistent attack   _____
11. Sifting utensil   _____
12. Man's first name   _____
13. Cooking surface with
    burners   _____
14. What Maleficent's raven
    became in the end   _____

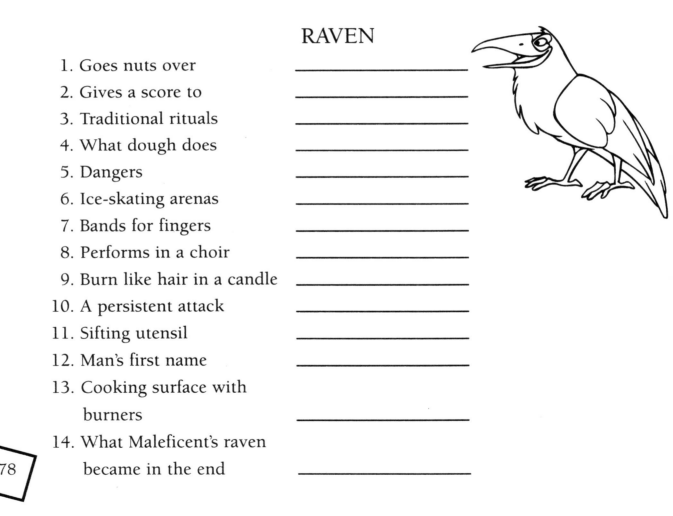

78

Answers on
page 164

Oh no! An old woman is trying to give Snow White a poisoned apple. The forest animals can sense that the old woman is really the evil Queen turned into a witch, and they are trying to warn Snow White.

Can you find at least eight birds, rabbits, and squirrels on this page?

79

Answers on page 164

Everyone at Ratcliffe's dinner table is at a different stage in his meal. Number the plates in order from the person who has eaten the least to the person who has eaten the most. (Assume that everyone started out with the same amount.) Then read the letters on the place cards in order from one to eight to find a bonus word.

80

Answers on
page 164

How well do you remember details? Study this picture of Banzai, Shenzi, and Ed for up to three minutes, then turn the page to test your memory.

Answers on
page 164

The eight questions below refer to the scene based on *The Lion King* on page 83. If you can answer five or more correctly, you have an incredible memory for detail.

1. What are the hyenas stalking?
2. Do all the hyenas have their noses down?
3. What is on the log at the lower left?
4. Which one of these things is not in the scene?

5. Is the sun on the right or left side of the scene?
6. How many trees are in the scene?
7. Are any bushes blooming?
8. What is in the air at the left-hand side of the picture?

Answers on page 164

Si and Am, the destructive cats from *Lady and the Tramp,* look almost identical—but not quite. Can you spot at least five differences between them?

Answers on
page 164

By Jove! Jafar has stolen the magic lantern from Aladdin. For his first wish, he's asked for a room full of things that begin with the letter *J*. There aren't a jillion of them—you should be joyful if you find at least 15.

CELL 1

Answers on page 165

85

Answers on
page 165

Beginning with the one-letter word defined below, work your way down the triangle, adding one new letter on each line. Can you fill in all the layers?

1. Me, myself

2. Exists

3. _____ Hiss (character from *Robin Hood* pictured below)

4. Come up, like the sun

5. Most cars have four

6. Shere Khan's marking

7. Captain Hook's crew

The triangle is filled in as:
I
I S
S I R
R I S E
T H R E E S
S T R I P E
P I R A T E S

86

Answers on page 165

Flotsam and Jetsam, Ursula's pet eels from *The Little Mermaid,* are sneaky and snaky creatures. Here, one is lying and one is telling the truth. Can you figure out which eel is which?

Jetsam's teeth are showing. I am telling the truth.

Flotsam is on the right. Jetsam is lying.

Answers on page 165

Match each set of letters from List A to a set from List B to form a new word. All the words will have something to do with *Beauty and the Beast*. You should be able to use all the letters.

LIST A

WAG
GAS
SUP
BOOKS
MANS
HAND
FAT
HA
PET

LIST B

TORE
SOME
TRACK
ALS
HER
ON
PER
ION
TON

88

Answers on page 165

The evil Cruella De Vil is driving around wildly searching for the Dalmatian puppies. Her henchmen, Horace and Jasper, are helping her. Can you follow the trails of smoke from Cruella's car and Horace and Jasper's truck and figure out where each of them started their drives?

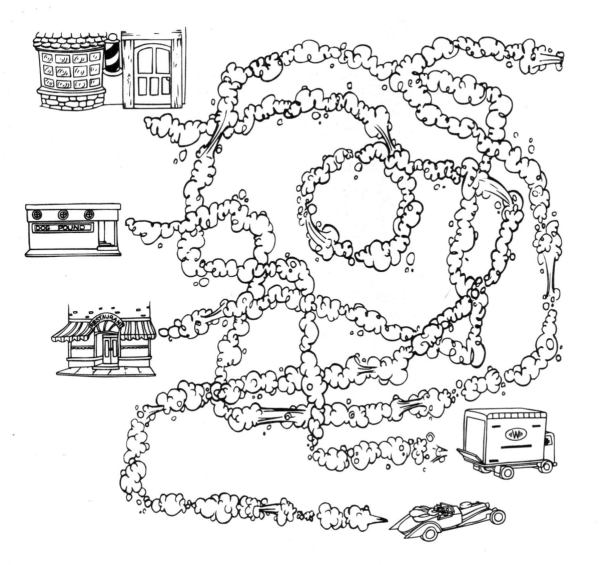

89

Answers on page 165

Answers on
page 165

Mowgli has tied a flaming branch to Shere Khan's tail,
and the tiger is running wildly through the jungle.
On the next page are several snapshots showing what
Shere Khan saw as he ran. Can you number them in the
order in which he saw them?

_____

_____

_____

_____

_____

_____

Answers on
page 165

Layered Lunch

Lampwick, Pinocchio's deviant pal, is helping himself to the world's largest sandwich. All the ingredients are hidden in the word search below. Can you find the 12 fillings? The words are hidden in straight lines across, back, up, down, and diagonally in the grid.

```
I  L  A  D  R  E  O  U  F  T  Y  S
M  C  B  H  O  H  O  T  D  O  G  P
I  L  E  O  T  D  G  K  N  C  O  R
A  P  I  C  K  L  E  C  A  T  R  E
K  N  I  L  R  P  H  I  O  G  K  G
L  C  G  K  L  E  I  T  N  A  N  O
E  T  T  O  E  N  A  S  C  T  B  L
T  U  C  S  L  M  N  M  U  S  A  R
T  I  E  A  O  O  A  U  C  D  N  D
U  M  N  T  L  A  B  R  R  O  A  O
C  B  A  H  A  M  U  D  S  T  N  B
E  A  D  R  A  T  S  U  M  A  A  E
```

BANANA
BOLOGNA
CAKE
CHEESE
DRUMSTICK
HAM

HOT DOG
ICE-CREAM CONE
LETTUCE
MUSTARD
PICKLE
TOMATO

92

Answers on page 166

How good is your memory? Study this scene based on *Snow White and the Seven Dwarfs* for up to three minutes, then turn the page to answer some questions about what you saw.

93

Answers on page 166

The eight questions below refer to the scene based on *Snow White and the Seven Dwarfs* on the previous page. If you can answer five or more correctly, your memory is crystal clear.

1. How many dwarfs are in the scene?
2. Does the witch have a wart?
3. Which of these trees is in the scene?

4. Which dwarf is first in line?
5. What does Doc have in his hand?
6. What is strange about the dwarf farthest to the right in the scene?
7. What is on the branch next to the witch?
8. What kind of animal is sitting on the rock near Doc?

94

Answers on page 166

Each of the six Disney characters below is different from all the others in at least one way. Can you pinpoint why each one stands alone? (In some cases, your answers may not be the same as ours.)

95

Answers on
page 166

Jafar's swordsmen are chasing Aladdin through the streets of Agrabah. A bird's-eye view of their trail is shown below. On the next page are several snapshots showing what Aladdin saw as he ran. Can you number them in the order in which he saw them?

Answers on
page 166

1 _____

3 _____

6 _____

4 _____

5 _____

2 _____

97

Answers on
page 166

Captain Hook has had his pirates line up to spell out a message for Peter Pan. Using the flag code (called "semaphore" by sailors) defined in the box on the right, can you read Hook's message?

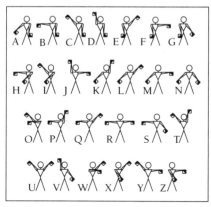

Answers on
page 166

Match each set of letters from List A to a set from List B to form a new word. All the words will have something to do with *The Lion King*. You should be able to use all the letters.

LIST A   LIST B

FEAT   ER
ANT   YON
STAM   HOG
MON   HER
WART   PEDE
POW   ELOPE
CAN   NESS
LIO   KEY

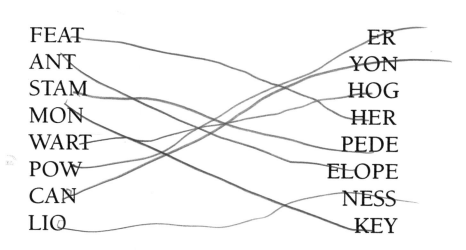

Answers on
page 166

The Queen in *Snow White and the Seven Dwarfs* uses a thunderbolt to mix a poison brew. All the words pictured below are spelled with only the letters in *THUNDERBOLT*. Can you identify all of them?

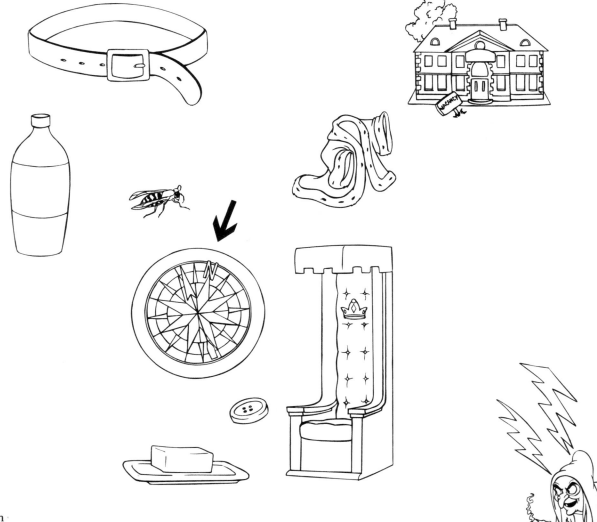

Answers on page 167

"Off with their heads!" shouts the Queen of Hearts to her card servants. "I want you to arrange yourselves in a more orderly fashion. Line up in four rows of four so that the total number of hearts in each row and column adds up to 20! And don't stop there—make the diagonals add up to 20, too!"

Can you satisfy the Queen's command?

Answers on page 167

In each of the lists below, the names of eight related things are listed in code—every letter of the alphabet has been replaced with a different letter. To break the code, substitute the letters from the answers given and try to figure out the rest of the answers. Can you break all four codes? (Remember, each list uses a different set of substitutions.)

1. TYPES OF CATS

A B C D
L I O N
‗ ‗ ‗ ‗

E B F G H
‗ ‗ ‗ ‗ ‗

A G C I J H K
‗ ‗ ‗ ‗ ‗ ‗ ‗

L C L M J E
‗ ‗ ‗ ‗ ‗ ‗

M C N F J H
‗ ‗ ‗ ‗ ‗ ‗

R J F N J H
‗ ‗ ‗ ‗ ‗ ‗

I J D E O G H
‗ ‗ ‗ ‗ ‗ ‗ ‗

A P D Q
‗ ‗ ‗ ‗

2. MEN'S NAMES THAT BEGIN WITH G

P R I H A W
G A S T O N
‗ ‗ ‗ ‗ ‗ ‗

P T A C P T
‗ ‗ ‗ ‗ ‗ ‗

P F U L T C H
‗ ‗ ‗ ‗ ‗ ‗ ‗

P A C X A W
‗ ‗ ‗ ‗ ‗ ‗

P R C J
‗ ‗ ‗ ‗

P C T P A C J
‗ ‗ ‗ ‗ ‗ ‗ ‗

P C R B R E
‗ ‗ ‗ ‗ ‗ ‗

P T S S T H H A
‗ ‗ ‗ ‗ ‗ ‗ ‗ ‗

Answers on
page 167

3. ROYALTY

Z G L L O
Q U E E N
<u>Q U E E N</u>

R D O B
— — — —

V U D O H L N N
— — — — — — — —

R O D B T Y
— — — — — —

A G H T L N N
— — — — — — —

F J U C O
— — — — —

H C G O Y
— — — — —

I J U Z G D N
— — — — — — —

4. SYNONYMS FOR *FOOL*

Y D K A D K
N I T W I T
<u>N I T W I T</u>

U D Y M O S K
— — — — — — —

V C G C Y
— — — — —

B D V E J H K C Y
— — — — — — — — —

D U D C K
— — — — —

U L Y F H
— — — — —

Y L V B I L J J
— — — — — — — —

O J C F I X H S U
— — — — — — — — —

Answers on page 167

When you finish this puzzle, you will have drawn a doggone despicable character from a Disney film. To find out who it is, draw what you see in box 3B into the square in row 3 and column B in the blank grid. Do the same with each square until all 15 boxes are filled in.

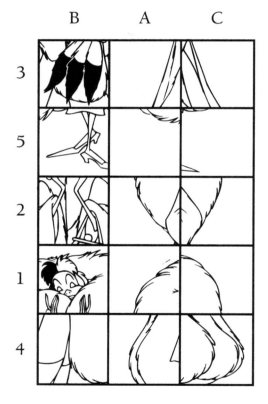

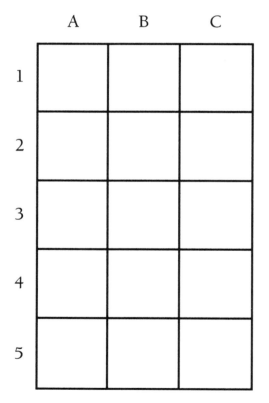

Answers on
page 168

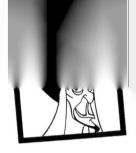

Answer the clues below and transfer the letters to the correspondingly numbered spaces at the bottom of the page to answer the following riddle:

When Jafar started flames burning and turned himself into a serpent, what did he want to do?

1. Word shouted to get assistance

$\overline{}$ $\overline{}$ $\overline{}$ $\overline{}$
10   15   4   6

2. Frozen drip of water

$\overline{}$ $\overline{}$ $\overline{}$ $\overline{}$ $\overline{}$ $\overline{}$
13   1   3   1   4   11

3. House____, horse____, or dragon____

$\overline{}$ $\overline{}$ $\overline{}$
12   4   8

4. Problem or mischief

$\overline{}$ $\overline{}$ $\overline{}$ $\overline{}$ $\overline{}$ $\overline{}$ $\overline{}$
9   14   2   5   7   4   15

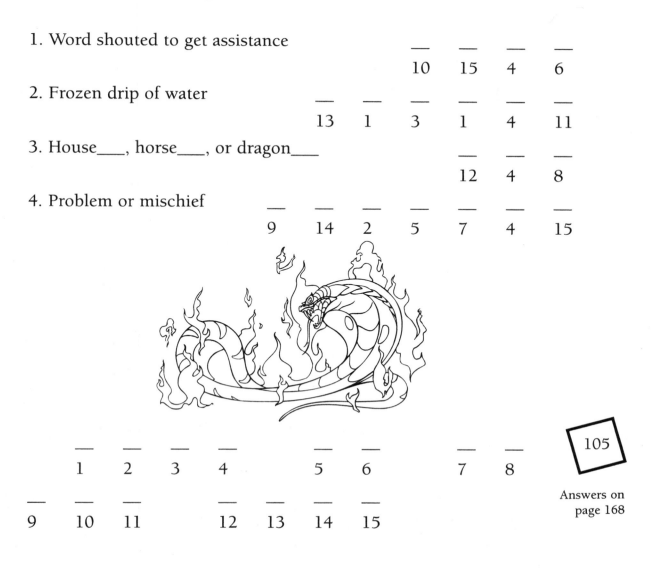

$\overline{}$ $\overline{}$ $\overline{}$ $\overline{}$ $\overline{}$ $\overline{}$ $\overline{}$ $\overline{}$
1   2   3   4   5   6   7   8

$\overline{}$ $\overline{}$ $\overline{}$ $\overline{}$ $\overline{}$ $\overline{}$ $\overline{}$
9   10   11   12   13   14   15

105

Answers on page 168

Answers on
page 168

There are at least 10 things wrong in this scene based on *Beauty and the Beast*. If you can find them all, you've got smashing skills of observation.

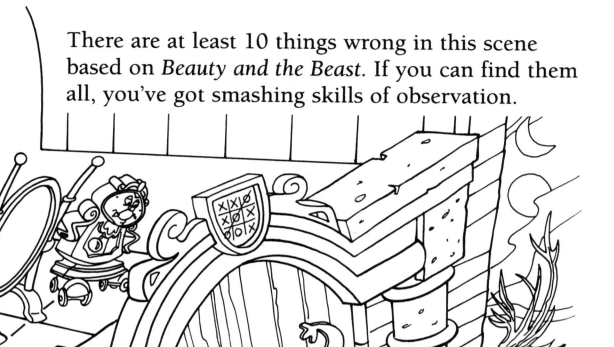

107

Answers on page 168

If three dogs can pull with the same force as two dogcatchers and two beavers can equal one dogcatcher, will these four dogcatchers be able to pull the four dogs and two beavers into the cage?

108

Answers on
page 168

Ursula the Sea Witch has whipped up a whirlpool with King Triton's trident. Ariel is being sucked into the middle of the whirlpool, along with many other objects. Can you unscramble the words below and find the items?

YILECCB
TOBELT
CROATR
GHSOODUE

EGLOGSG
MUREPJOP
ALPM
ONIPA

109

Answers on page 169

Twelve words that rhyme with *goon* are defined below.
Can you figure out every one?

1. Summer month   _____

2. Mountain of sand   _____

3. Helium-filled toy   _____

4. Comic strip   _____

5. Dried plum   _____

6. Twelve o'clock, midday   _____

7. Big primate   _____

8. "Masked" mammal   _____

9. Soup utensil   _____

10. Deep red color   _____

11. Deep woodwind instrument   _____

12. Shallow pond off the sea   _____

110

Answers on
page 169

There are 10 differences between these two scenes based on *The Lion King.* Can you spot them all?

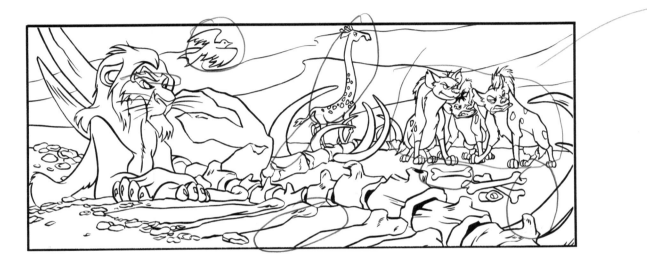

Answers on page 169

Aladdin is being held in the Sultan's dungeon. He has been chained up so long that he's seeing images in the cracks in the walls. Color in every section of the wall that contains exactly two dots and you'll see an image, too.

Answers on page 169

Sneaky Snakes

Kaa is all in a tangle over this list of his cousins. Can you straighten out the letters in each line to spell the name of a type of snake?

1. OAB — Boa

2. SAP — Asp

3. DREAD — _____

4. CAROB — _____

5. PRIVE — _____

6. GARRET — _____

7. PHOTYN — _____

8. ONCANADA — _____

9. WISERIDDEN — _____

10. LOCAR KEANS — _____

11. PEACHPRODE — _____

12. KNEESTARTAL — _____

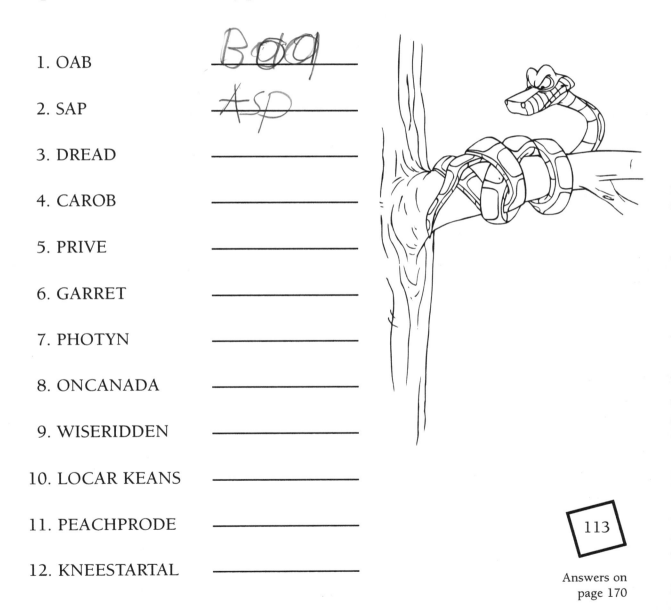

113

Answers on page 170

Settled Settler

Ratcliffe's well-equipped tent is shown below. Use the numbers next to some of the objects to solve the picture crossword below. For example, 1 Across is *BATHTUB*.

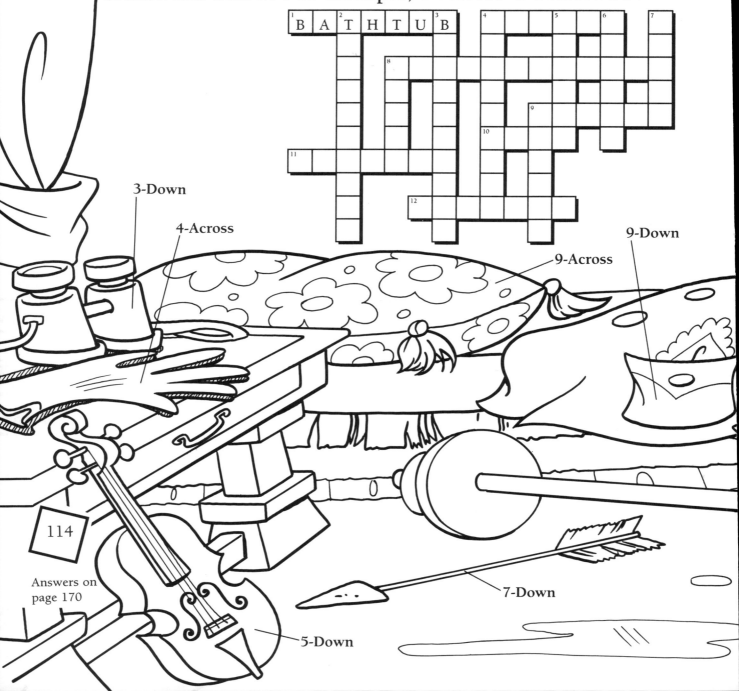

3-Down

4-Across

9-Across

9-Down

7-Down

5-Down

114

Answers on page 170

8-Down

10-Across

2-Down

6-Down

8-Across

11-Across

1-Across

12-Across

4-Down

115

Answers on page 170

Captain Hook's first mate, Smee, has been noticing a lot of things on the pirate ship that rhyme with his name. Can you find at least nine things in this scene that rhyme with *SMEE*?

Answers on
page 170

What is appearing in the Queen's mirror? To find out, connect the dots from 1 to 30. (Hint: It's the fairest one of all.)

Answers on
page 170

Invite Tease

The invitation below is either for Lady Tremaine or one of her daughters, Anastasia or Drizella. But the messenger isn't being straight about who it's for. Can you use his clues to figure out who is invited to the prince's ball?

The king requests the presence of the one of you who plays violin. The king is aware that Anastasia is wearing earrings that match her mother's, that Drizella has never touched a stringed instrument, and that the invitee is not wearing a beaded bracelet.

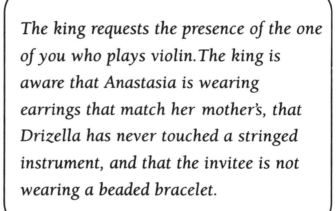

Answers on page 170

Tramp is chasing rats out of Lady's house, where they might disturb the baby. Can you start where Tramp is and get through the maze and out the door, tracing over all the rats and not using any segment of the maze more than once?

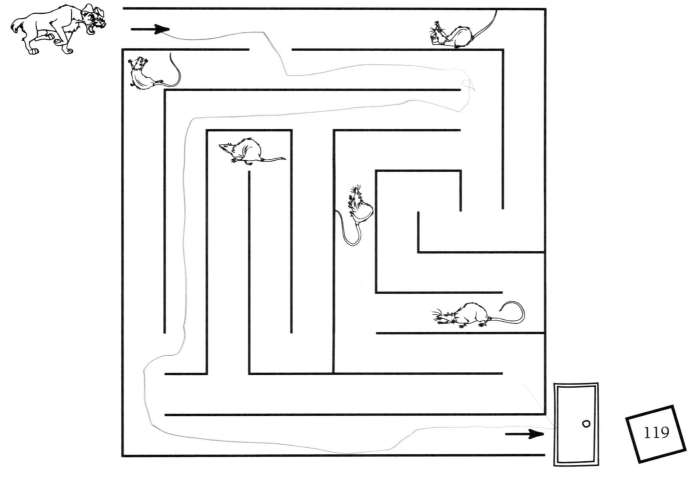

119

Answers on page 171

MOVIE
MIX

Each of the crosswords on these two pages is made up of a set of related words. We've given you the category and some of the letters as a guide. Can you complete the grids?

1. BLACK THINGS

URSULA sees where her name fits in the grid. Can you write in the other black things?

2. SHADES OF RED

The Queen of Hearts sees where *CRIMSON* goes. What are the other shades of red?

120

Answers on page 171

3. VEHICLES

Lady Tremaine found her *COACH* in the grid. What other forms of transportation are here?

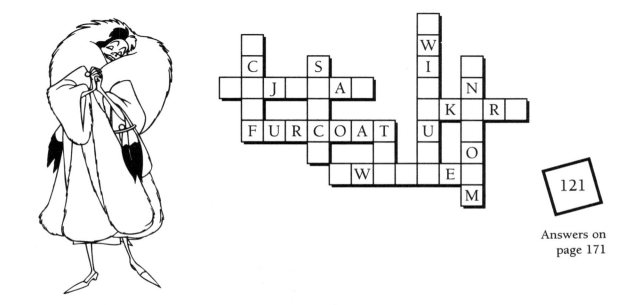

4. CLOTHING

Cruella De Vil has spotted *FUR COAT* in the grid. Can you fill in the rest?

121

Answers on page 171

There are some camels and some people in the market square. Jafar counted 46 feet and 18 heads. How many camels are there? How many people?

Answers on page 172

Stromboli tells Pinocchio that he'll be famous one day. To find out his exact words, answer the seven clues below. Then write each letter in the matching numbered box at the bottom of the page to spell out Stromboli's comment.

1. Up-and-down toy on a string

— — - — —
1 15 21 28

2. Retaliation

— — — — — — —
4 32 18 8 29 30 14

3. The three pigs met a big bad one

— — — —
9 2 12 5

4. What you should do before a test

— — — — —
26 27 31 24 25

5. Birch-bark boat

— — — — —
7 6 16 23 17

6. The part that lights up when you turn on a lamp

— — — —
22 3 11 13

7. Anger

— — —
10 20 19

"
— — — — — — — —
1 2 3 4   5 6 7 8

— — — — — — — —
9 10 11 12   13 14   15 16
                          ,
— — — — — — — — — —
17 18 19 20 21 22 23 24 25 26
                    "
— — — — — —
27 28 29 30 31 32

Answers on page 172

Cruella De Vil is searching for the Dalmatian puppies, but they've covered themselves in soot. On this page there are three pairs of identical puppies. Can you find them?

Answers on
page 172

Ursula the conniving Sea Witch gave Ariel three days to get Eric to kiss her. Calculate how much time she's spent so far and then figure out if she still has time left before her soul becomes Ursula's forever.

Ariel spent 10 hours swimming to shore.

She was onshore half again that long before someone found her.

She spent one-quarter of a day getting ready for dinner and eating.

Ariel and Eric went for a four-hour carriage ride.

Ariel slept twice for one-third of a day each time.

She walked around the town and asked for advice from friends for half a day.

She saw Ursula disguised as a young woman and spent half a day planning what she could do to expose her.

Ariel spent six hours getting onto Eric's boat and carrying out her plan.

Has Ariel run out of time?

125

Answers on
page 172

Can you draw two straight lines to divide these hyenas into four groups? Each group must have the same number of hyenas facing right as facing left—but each group may have a different total number of hyenas.

Answers on
page 172

Gaston has fallen in the mud after proposing to Belle. Which of the boxes at the bottom of the page is taken exactly from the scene?

A

B

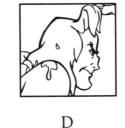

C

D

MIX

In each of the lists below, the names of eight related things are listed in code—every letter of the alphabet has been replaced with a different letter. To break the code, substitute the letters from the answers given and try to figure out the rest of the answers. Can you break all four codes? (Remember, each list uses a different set of substitutions.)

1. SYNONYMS FOR UGLY

A B C D E F G
H I D E O U S
‾ ‾ ‾ ‾ ‾ ‾ ‾

H D I F J G B K D
‾ ‾ ‾ ‾ ‾ ‾ ‾ ‾ ‾

F L G B M A N J O
‾ ‾ ‾ ‾ ‾ ‾ ‾ ‾ ‾

C H D P C Q F J
‾ ‾ ‾ ‾ ‾ ‾ ‾ ‾

M H F D G E R D
‾ ‾ ‾ ‾ ‾ ‾ ‾ ‾

M A P G N J O
‾ ‾ ‾ ‾ ‾ ‾ ‾

Q H B M A N Q F J
‾ ‾ ‾ ‾ ‾ ‾ ‾ ‾ ‾

M H E N D G S F D
‾ ‾ ‾ ‾ ‾ ‾ ‾ ‾ ‾

2. BIG ANIMALS

E N O R M
W H A L E
‾ ‾ ‾ ‾ ‾

M R M U N O W V
‾ ‾ ‾ ‾ ‾ ‾ ‾ ‾

A S O W V   V B L V B S C M
‾ ‾ ‾ ‾   ‾ ‾ ‾ ‾ ‾ ‾ ‾

A S L O G G M
‾ ‾ ‾ ‾ ‾ ‾ ‾

C M O   R S B W
‾ ‾ ‾   ‾ ‾ ‾ ‾

D O D D B V N
‾ ‾ ‾ ‾ ‾ ‾ ‾

L N S W B H M L   B C
‾ ‾ ‾ ‾ ‾ ‾ ‾ ‾   ‾ ‾

A L S F   F R T   I M O L
‾ ‾ ‾ ‾   ‾ ‾ ‾   ‾ ‾ ‾ ‾

Answers on
page 173

3. BIRDS

I K N N C E
P A R R O T
— — — — — —

C Q E N T Y M
— — — — — —

I G K Y C Y Z
— — — — — — —

M A W W T O B F T N L
— — — — — — — — — — —

J A R E A N G
— — — — — — —

I G R T Y K O
— — — — — — —

D C C L I G Y Z G N
— — — — — — — — — —

F R A G H K P
— — — — — — —

4. BLACK AND WHITE

T H E X   H D F H B
D A L M A T I A N
— — — — — — — — —

C Y G M H
— — — — —

A K Y A N Y M G W H M T
— — — — — — — — — — — —

W E T   X W I F Y P
— — —   — — — — — —

P N Q B N
— — — — —

Z F H B W   N Y L P
— — — — —   — — — —

W B Y - O H L   P F J B
— — — - — — —   — — — —

Z Y B J Q F B
— — — — — — —

Answers on
page 173

One of Alice's scariest experiences in Wonderland was growing larger than a house. There are several things besides Alice that are not in proportion to the White Rabbit's house in the scene below. Can you find five other things that are too big or too small compared with the house?

Answers on
page 173

Iago is hiding among the flamingos, imitating Jasmine's voice to lure Aladdin away from the lamp. Can you find *IAGO* hidden across, back, up, down, or diagonally in the flamingos below? His name is hidden only once.

```
F L A M I N G O F N
A I L A O I N L O G
M L A F G N A I O A
I N G G O M I N G O
F G O F I G O F A G
L I A N I M A L I N
N A G I M A L F N I
A O A L A N G L A M
G N I M F A O N G O
I A O G N I M A L F
```

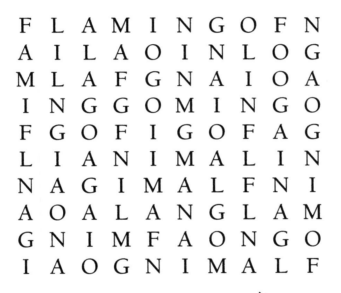

131

Answers on page 174

Robin Hood is disguised as one of the archers below. Prince John is trying to figure out which one. A few of the contestants have given him the clues below. Can you figure out which archer is really Robin Hood?

When you finish this puzzle, you'll have drawn a scary character from a Disney film. To find out who it is, draw what you see in box 3B into the square in row 3 and column B in the blank grid. Do the same with each square until all 12 boxes are filled in.

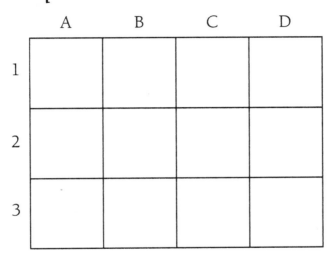

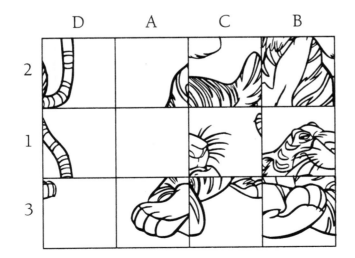

Answers on page 174

The names of 11 kinds of fruit are mixed into the evil Queen's poison potion below. We've circled one—*grape*—as an example. Can you find the rest? All the letters in each word are linked in a chain, and all the letters will be used.

R E H C P I N E
R M I E L P P A
Y E L G L E M O
A E P R A P E N
C A A T C E N A
H P R I N O C P
P P L E E T I R
L U M M A N G O

Answers on
page 174

Scar has assembled an army of hyenas. How many do you think there are? To figure it out, use the formula below.

1. Take three times the number of Scar's paws ____
2. Multiply by one-half the number of bones in the scene ____
3. Add Scar's age times two ____

<u>To find Scar's age:</u>

Scar was injured when he was two years old, giving him the scar above his left eye.
He has had the scar for two-thirds of his life.

135

Answers on page 174

Gaston thinks he's the champion of all sports. The answers to the rebuses below are all words that concern one particular sport. Can you solve the picture puzzles and figure out which sport?

To solve a rebus, add and subtract the letters of the words that are illustrated as shown.

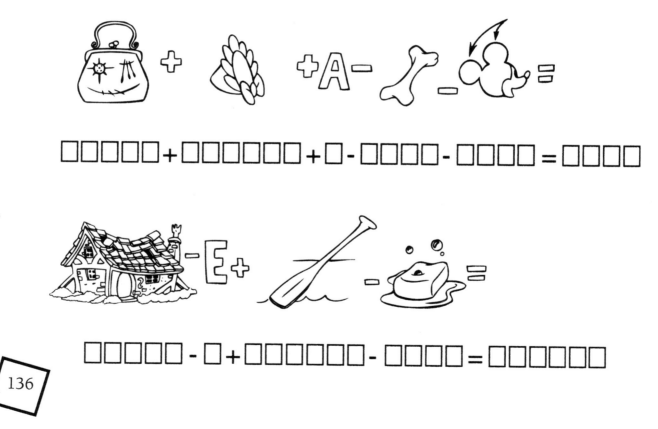

□□□□ + □□□ + □□□□□□ - □□□□□□ - □□□ = □□□□

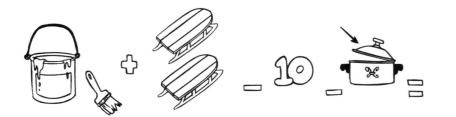

□□□□□ + □□□□□ - □□□ - □□□ = □□□□

Answers on
page 174

Armed with Words

Most of the things pictured on this page can be spelled using only the letters in the word *TENTACLES*. One object is spelled with a letter that is not in the word *TENTACLES*. Can you find it? Also, how many other words of four or more letters can you spell from *TENTACLES*? You may only use a letter twice if it appears twice in *TENTACLES* (like *E*).

Double Vision IV

There are 10 differences between these two scenes based on *Cinderella*. Can you spot them all?

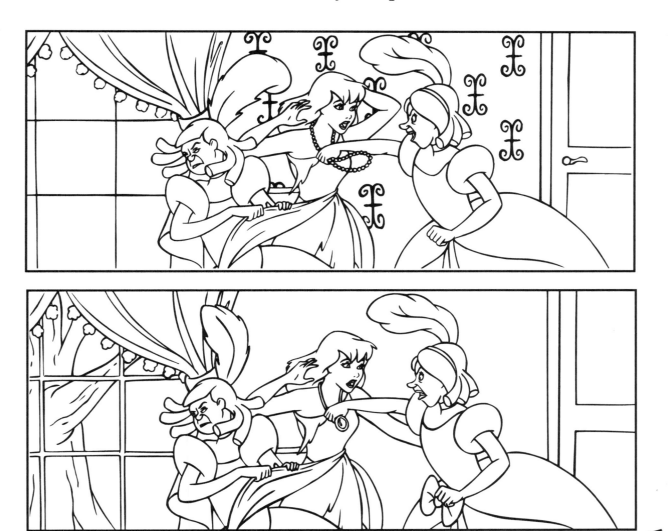

139

Answers on page 175

The *I*'s Have It

I's are the only vowels in Wiggins's name. All the words and phrases defined below also contain no other vowels but *I*'s. How many can you *ID*?

1. Electric flash during a thunderstorm   _____

2. Makeup for the mouth   _____

3. Band worn on the smallest finger   _____

4. Machine that makes power from breezes   _____

5. Last six outs of a baseball game   _____

6. Chair taken up a snowy mountain   _____

7. Pinocchio's friend ___ Cricket   _____

8. U.S. state, home of Jackson and Biloxi   _____

9. Two-piece swimsuit   _____

Answers on page 175

Look at these dogs in the pound in *Lady and the Tramp*. There is a pattern in the way they're lined up. Which of the three dogs at the bottom of the page should go next?

1

2

3

4

5

6

Answers on
page 175

Jafar and Iago are brewing up some evil deeds. There are five magic lamps hidden in this scene, along with the two halves of Jafar's charm. Can you find them all?

142

Answers on
page 175

143

Although Ed never speaks except to laugh, he's collected a list of 12 words that rhyme with his name. How many can you figure out?

1. Color of tomatoes   _____
2. Drove too fast   _____
3. Ran away   _____
4. Rye or sourdough   _____
5. Toboggan   _____
6. Ridge on tires or shoes   _____
7. Finished a book   _____
8. Topmost body part   _____
9. Gave food to   _____
10. Furniture to sleep on   _____

Answers on page 176

Home Run

Can you get the Dalmatian puppies safely home without running into Cruella De Vil, Horace, or Jasper?

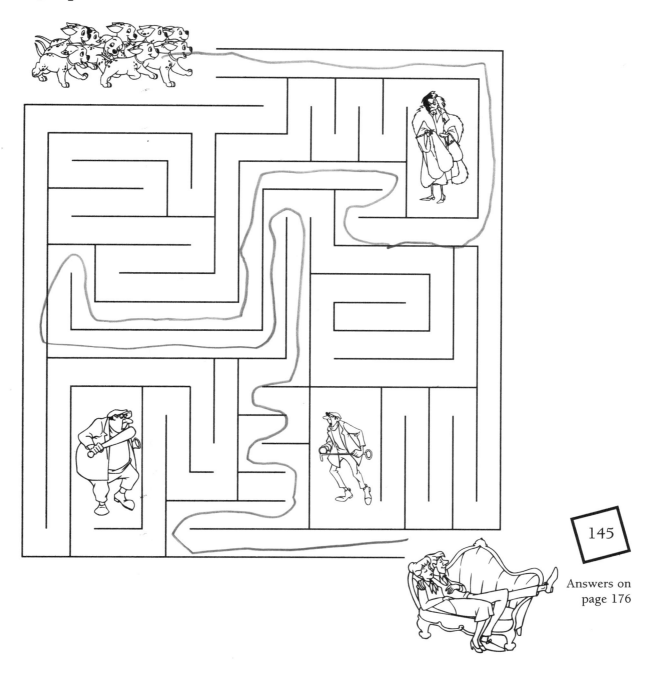

145

Answers on page 176

Villain Vexation

All the Disney villains listed here can fit into the grid at right. *MALEFICENT* and *GIDEON* are filled in to get you started. Using the lengths of the words and the letters that are in place, can you fill in the rest of the names? (Note: There is no space between words in the grid. For example, Captain Hook is *CAPTAINHOOK* in the grid.)

ANASTASIA	GOONS	SHENZI
BANZAI	HORACE BADUN	SHERE KHAN
BRUTUS	JAFAR	SI
CAPTAIN HOOK	JASPER	SIR HISS
COACHMAN	JETSAM	SMEE
DRIZELLA	MALEFICENT	SNOOPS
ED	MEDUSA	STROMBOLI
FLOTSAM	NERO	URSULA
GASTON	PRINCE JOHN	WITCH
GIDEON	RAVEN	

Answers on page 176

M A L E F I C E N T

G I D E O N

147

Answers on
page 176

ANSWERS

7 Lurking Evil

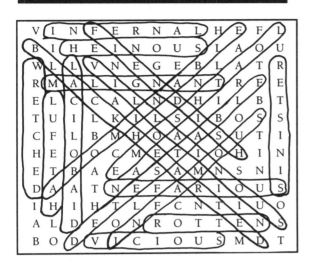

8 Silly Safari

1. Zazu has a banana for a beak;
2. The zebra's stripes are going the wrong way;   3. There's a bicycle leaning against the tree;   4. The snake has two tails;   5. The ostrich has rabbit ears;   6. The giraffe's legs are too short;   7. The hyena has three hind legs;   8. The elephant is in a hole;   9. There are two suns in the sky;   10. One wildebeest is walking with a cane

9 Stormy Weather

1. Rain
2. Hail
3. Fire
4. Flood
5. Sleet
6. Volcano
7. Monsoon
8. Drought
9. Thunder
10. Tornado
11. Blizzard
12. Mudslide
13. Hurricane
14. Earthquake

10 Wicked Witchery

Wall, wart, watch, wax (candle), web, well, wheelbarrow, whistle, wick, window, windowsill, wing, wishbone, witch, wood, wrench, wrist

12 Aim to Win

Gaston's darts must land on **50**, **10**, **5**, **3**, and **1** (50 + 10 + 5 + 3 + 1 = 69)

149

ANSWER
PAGE

13 Knot Allowed

Snake B will make a knot if you pulled his head and tail. The other two will not

14 Matchmaker I

The bonus word is **trouble**

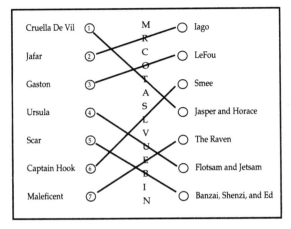

15 Double Vision I

1. Ursula's hair is missing a section in the bottom scene; **2.** The bones on the fish pen are pointing in different directions; **3.** Ursula's dress has straps in the bottom scene; **4.** The top eel is facing in different directions; **5.** The lower eel's eyes are looking in different directions; **6.** There's an extra plant behind the lost souls in the bottom scene; **7.** One of the souls is missing in the bottom scene; **8.** The plant on the far right has one leaf bent in the bottom scene; **9.** The bottom eel's top scales are different; **10.** The tentacle over Ursula's shoulder is not colored in in the top scene

16 Deep Trouble

17 Stately Names

1. Did you see the *Queen **Mary** land*? (MARYLAND)
2. The Swiss **miss is sipp**ing hot cocoa. (MISSISSIPPI)
3. Johnny, it is okay to **color a do**nkey green. (COLORADO)
4. Be sure to correctly match cities to states; Den**ver, Mont**ana, is incorrect. (VERMONT)
5. When the tide comes in, is the sh**ore gon**e? (OREGON)
6. Rad**io wa**ves can travel farther at night. (IOWA)
7. I want to redecorate in sal**mon, tan, a**nd olive. (MONTANA)
8. Are you doing the **washing ton**ight or tomorrow? (WASHINGTON)
9. **Oh! I o**nly bought enough popcorn for two. (OHIO)
10. Anita—who h**id a ho**rse in Harold's house? (IDAHO)

18 Coin Collectors

Ratcliffe and Wiggins should bring bags **A** and **D**

20 Surrounded

Hyenas **A** and **D** are exactly alike

21 Take-Outs I

Box C is taken directly from the scene

19 Quick Draw I

Your drawing should look like this:

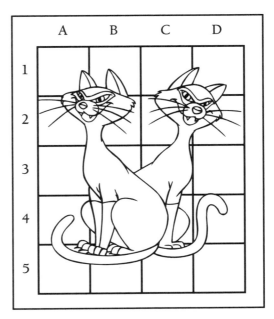

151

22 Cross Roads

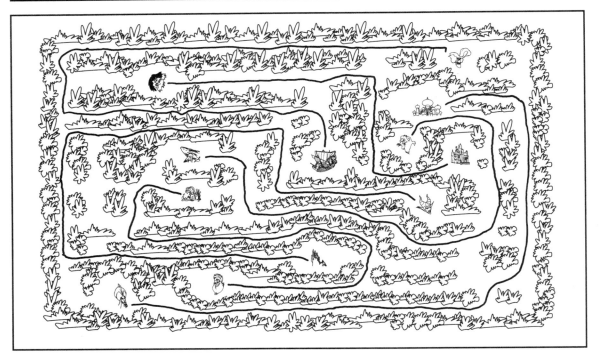

24 Dug Out

If you've followed the directions exactly, you will end up back at the cave entrance. The treasure is buried there

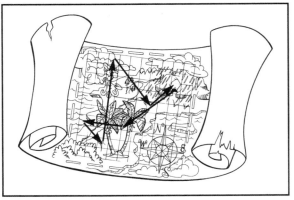

25 Ten Tons

1. Tongue
2. Stone
3. Tonight
4. Baton
5. Futon
6. Carton
7. Button
8. Cotton
9. Washington, D.C.
10. Tetons

26 Image Problems

1. Sebastian is reflected at the porthole instead of Scuttle; 2. The hat rack is reflected as a cactus; 3. The coat hanging on the hat rack is different;.
4. The empty hanger on the hat rack is different; 5. The cloud in the sky in the window is a different shape; 6. The necklace on the edge of the table is not reflected; 7. The comb is reflected as a perfume bottle; 8. The other two bottles on the table are reflected incorrectly; 9. Ursula's hand is in a different position on the table; 10. The chair Ursula is sitting on is different

27 Ready, Aim . . .

1. No, Ratcliffe is not holding a weapon; 2. Percy is hiding behind the fence on the right; 3. A campfire; 4. The first box is not in the scene;
5. Seven; 6. A British flag; 7. A portrait of King James; 8. A fence

29 Block Head

Alice should choose **stack F**

30 Strike Alikes

All six swordsmen are wearing the same kind of shoes

153

31 Dark Spot

1. Uniform
2. Forest
3. Band
4. Domino

The answer is **Forbidden Mountains**

32 Through the Cracks

It's **a snake**

33 Word Hound

Aced, acre, actor, aged, arched, cage, card, care, cargo, cart, catch, charge, chart, cheat, chord, coach, coat, code, cold, core, crag, crate, dare, dart, date, dearth, death, doer, each, earth, echo, ergo, etch, gate, gather, goad, goat, gore, grace, grade, grate, great, hare, hate, head, heard, heart, heat, herd, hoard, ocher (ochre), ogre, order, other, race, rage, rate, reach, react, read, roach, road, rode, rote, taco, teach, tear, toad, torch, trace, tread

34 Canine Rebuses

1. COmb + YOlk + Tie - milk - b = **COYOTE**
2. barn + DOor + LEG - barrel - no = **DOG**
3. sWOrd + pen + LeaF - pans - deer = **WOLF**
4. FlOwer + tooth + siX - whistle - root = **FOX**

36 Mini-Crosswords I

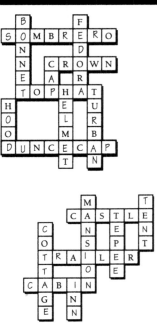

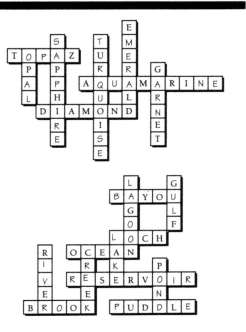

38 Fishing Lines

39 Kingdom Come

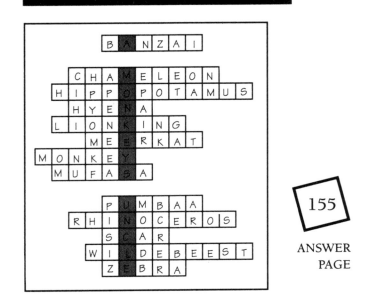

40 Dirty Pool

Three solid balls and two striped balls will go in. Therefore, **Pinocchio** will sink more balls

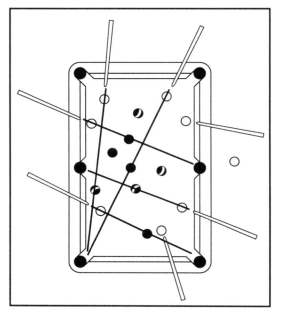

41 Gold Mine

1. Mule
2. Glove
3. Teeth
4. Shark
5. Shower
6. Shade

Jafar's rule is, **Whoever has the gold makes the rules**

42 *S Curves*

Sack, safe, sail, scale, scallop (or shell), scarf, screwdriver, scroll, seagull, seven (on sweater), shark, shirt, shoes, sign, skate, skis, sleeve, slingshot, slot, snail, soap, sock (or stocking), sponge, spoon, starfish, statue, steps, sticks, stool, sweater, sword

44 Body Check

It's **a bird**

45 Where, Oh, Where

The dog is the oldest, and therefore the puppies are hiding with him

46 Royal Letters

Chin, chip, chirp, choir, chop, chore, cipher, coin, core, corn, crone, echo, hire, hone, hope, horn, icon, inch, inner, iron, join, neon, nicer, niche, nine, once, open, perch, phone, pier, pinch, pine, porch, pore, price, prone, rein, rice, rich, ripe, rope

47 On Track

The correct order is **1.** Horse and wagon; **2.** Maurice; **3.** Bird; **4.** Wolf; **5.** Beast; **6.** Belle

48 Shipmates

All six pirates are wearing the same kind of belt

49 Square Dances

51 BANned Words

1. Banana
2. Suburban
3. Bandage
4. Banister
5. Piggy bank
6. Banjo
7. Cuban
8. Banquet
9. Turban
10. Bandit

50 Double Vision II

1. Dumbo has no eyelashes in the top scene; 2. Skinny's hat is different; 3. Dumbo's toes are missing in the top scene; 4. There's a peanut on the floor behind Dumbo in the top scene; 5. Skinny's coat pocket is missing in the bottom scene; 6. The boy on the left is missing a section of his hair in the bottom scene; 7. The boy on the right has his baseball cap turned to the front in the bottom scene; 8. There is no straw in the cup in the top scene; 9. The boy on the right has buckles on his shoes in the bottom scene; 10. The boy on the left has his left hand in a different position

52 Hair Cuts

1F, 2E, 3G, 4D, 5B, 6C 7H, 8A

54 Stop, Thief!

Jafar can catch Aladdin stealing on **the 3rd**

55 Take-Outs II

Box A is taken directly from the scene

56 Hot Air

It's **a hot air balloon**

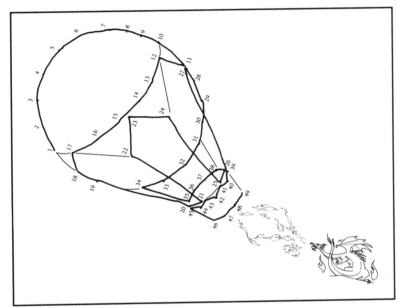

57 Two by Fours

$2 + 2 - 2 \div 2 = 1$
$2 - 2 \times 2 + 2 = 2$
$2 \times 2 + 2 \div 2 = 3$
$2 \div 2 \times 2 \times 2 = 4$
$2 \div 2 + 2 + 2 = 5$
$2 + 2 \times 2 - 2 = 6$
$2 + 2 + 2 + 2 = 8$

58 Silence!

1. Comb
2. Science
3. Wednesday
4. Eight
5. Ghost
6. Knot
7. Salmon
8. Column
9. Raspberry
10. Ballet
11. Who

159

ANSWER PAGE

59 Dogs Gone

60 Symbol Crash

PIG	FROG	WOLF	PORCUPINE	ROOSTER
ROOSTER	WOLF	PORCUPINE	PIG	FROG
PORCUPINE	ROOSTER	FROG	WOLF	PIG
FROG	PORCUPINE	PIG	ROOSTER	WOLF
WOLF	PIG	ROOSTER	FROG	PORCUPINE

61 Match Maker II

The bonus word is **bewitched**

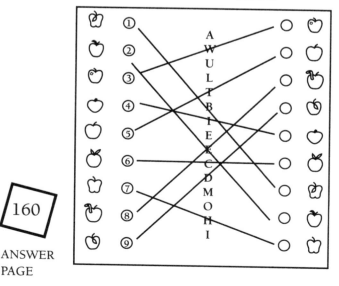

62 Wrong Doings

1. There's a basketball hoop on one of the trees; 2. Bagheera has whiskers on only one side of his face; 3. There are grapes coming out of a coconut; 4. Mowgli's right arm is too long; 5. There's a door in the tree by Mowgli; 6. One of the elephants is going the wrong way; 7. The shadows are going the wrong way; 8. There are bananas growing out of the ground; 9. The horizon doesn't match up behind the large tree; 10. Shere Khan''s tail isn't attached to his body

64 Three-for-All

1.
G	P	A	O	F	M
U	**R**	S	U	**L**	**A**
M	O	K	T	Y	D

2.
A	Z	U	S	H	I
G	**A**	S	**T**	O	**N**
E	P	E	Y	G	N

3.
I	J	A	T	O	D	I	K	E	A
M	**A**	**L**	**E**	**F**	**I**	**C**	**E**	**N**	**T**
P	M	L	E	F	M	E	Y	D	E

65 String Figure

Stromboli's puppet looks just like him!

66 Manhunt

161

ANSWER
PAGE

67 MINi ExaMINation

1. Mint
2. Minute
3. Domino
4. Vitamins
5. Flamingo
6. Benjamin
7. Aluminum
8. Miniature
9. Minnesota
10. Mincemeat

68 Different Folks I

Beginning at the top and going clockwise: only one settler has a mustache; only one settler doesn't have a shovel; only one settler is lying down; only one settler is frowning; only one settler is wearing a hat; only one settler is fat (You may find other reasons that some are different — there can be more than one correct answer!)

69 Time-Out

It's **11:45**

70 Vanishing Valuables

Vacuum, valentine, van, vane, vase, vault, vegetables, veil, vest, videos, Viking, villain (Ursula), violets, violin, viper, vise, visor, voice (Ariel's voice is trapped in Ursula's necklace), volcano, volleyball, volumes (books), vowels, vulture

72 Letter Juggler

1. Words/sword
2. Rats/star
3. Sneak/snake
4. Gum/mug
5. Shore/horse

162

73 Board Walk

It's **a skull and crossbones**

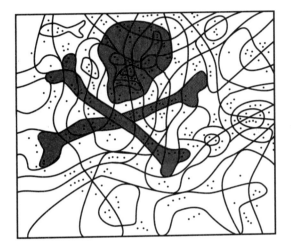

74 Quick Draw II

Your drawing should look like this:

75 Beast Quest

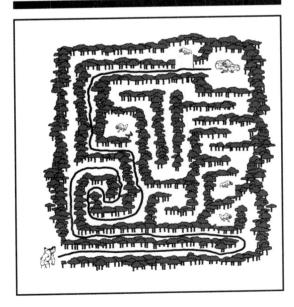

76 Wreck Room

1. Cruella is wearing two different shoes; 2. The clock face is upside down; 3. The curtain is outside the window; 4. There's a poetry book on the piano; 5. The piano bench's legs don't match; 6. The fringe on the rug doesn't go all the way around; 7. The light beside the doorway is a pencil; 8. The dogs' spots continue on the wall behind Pongo and Perdita; 9. "Dictionary" is spelled wrong; 10. There's a flower growing out of the television antenna

78 Letter for Letter

1. Raves
2. Rates
3. Rites
4. Rises
5. Risks
6. Rinks
7. Rings
8. Sings
9. Singe
10. Siege
11. Sieve
12. Steve
13. Stove
14. Stone

79 Hidden Helpers

80 Food Order

Beginning at the bottom left, the correct answers are **M7**, **E2**, **L4**, **E8**, **T5**, **M1**, **A3**, **I6**

The bonus word is **mealtime**

81 Hyena Hunt

1. They're stalking each other
2. No
3. A mouse
4. The first box is not from the scene
5. Right
6. Three
7. Yes
8. Zazu

83 Siamese Twins

1. The cats' right ears are different;   2. The cat on the right has more whiskers;
3. The cats' front feet are in different positions;   4. The cats' tails are turned in different directions;   5. The markings on the cats' front leg are different;
6. The cat on the left has its back claws showing

84 *J* Walking

Jack, jack-in-the-box, jack-o'-lantern, jacks, Jafar, jaguar, jail, jars, Jasmine, javelin, jay, jelly, jellyfish, jester, jet, jewelry, jig, jockey, jouster, judge, jug, juggler, July (on calendar), jump rope, jury, jury box

87 Truth Be Told

Jetsam is on the left—he is lying

89 Driven Crazy

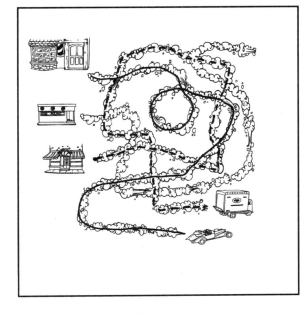

86 Word Triangle

1. I
2. Is
3. Sir
4. Rise
5. Tires
6. Stripe
7. Pirates

88 Word Binder I

Wagon
Gaston
Supper
Bookstore
Mansion
Handsome
Father
Hat Rack
Petals

90 Flaming Mad

1. Vultures; 2. Baloo the bear;
3. Kaa the snake; 4. Dancing monkeys; 5. King Louie the orangutan; 6. Mowgli

165

ANSWER PAGE

92 Layered Lunch

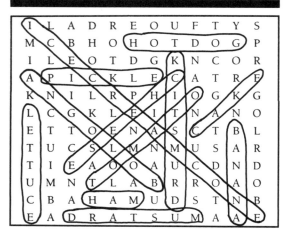

93 Witch Watch

1. Four
2. No
3. The second tree appears in the scene
4. Dopey
5. A club
6. Dopey is riding backward
7. A vulture
8. A squirrel

95 Different Folks II

Jafar is the only one sitting down; Maleficent is the only one who is female; Gaston is the only one facing left; Captain Hook is the only one not holding anything; Pinocchio is the only one who is not a villain; Prince John is the only one not gesturing

96 Chase Scene

1. The women in the window;
2. The snake charmer; 3. The fancy doorway; 4. The man sleeping on the bed of nails; 5. The fire breather; 6. The man walking on hot coals

98 Sign Language

Hook's message is, **Pan—I'll make you too sore to soar!**

99 Word Binder II

Feather
Antelope
Stampede
Monkey
Warthog
Power
Canyon
Lioness

100 Evil Spells

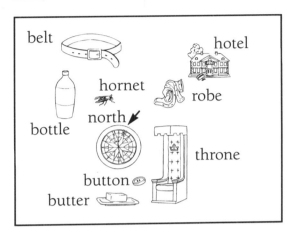

belt
hotel
hornet
robe
bottle
north
button
throne
butter

101 By Order of the Queen

This is one possible solution. You may be able to work out a different one.

2	6	8	4
7	4	3	6
6	8	5	1
5	2	4	9

102 Code Names I

1. TYPES OF CATS
Lion
Tiger
Leopard
Bobcat
Cougar
Jaguar
Panther
Lynx

2. MEN'S NAMES THAT BEGIN WITH G
Gaston
George
Gilbert
Gordon
Gary
Gregory
Graham
Geppetto

3. ROYALTY
Queen
King
Princess
Knight
Duchess
Baron
Count
Marquis

4. SYNONYMS FOR FOOL
Nitwit
Dingbat
Moron
Simpleton
Idiot
Dunce
Numskull

167

ANSWER PAGE

104 Quick Draw III

Your drawing should look like this:

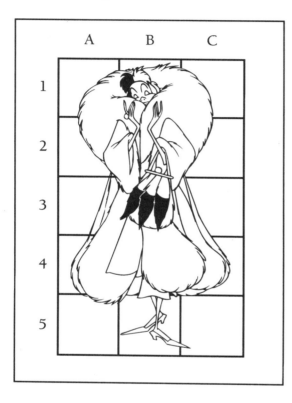

105 Snake Charmer

1. Help
2. Icicle
3. Fly
4. Trouble

The answer is **Coil up by the fire**

106 Crash Test

1. There is water running down the stairs; 2. One of the stair runners is a snake; 3. The picture on the wall is bursting out of its frame; 4. The clock face reads 13; 5. Cogsworth is on roller skates; 6. There's a leaf sprouting out of one of Lumiere's candles; 7. There are two kinds of plants growing out of the same stalk; 8. The mop is going through the dresser drawer; 9. There's a basketball where a globe should be; 10. The trunk is a doghouse; 11. LeFou is holding flowers instead of a torch; 12. One of the invaders has wheels instead of legs; 13. The footstool has spots; 14. There's a tic-tac-toe board above the door; 15. There are two moons in the sky

108 Pulling Strings

Yes: Each dogcatcher can pull 2 beavers, or 1 1/2 dogs. Four dogcatchers equal 8 beavers or 6 dogs. Therefore, they can outpull 2 beavers and 4 dogs.

109 Spin Cycle

Bicycle, bottle, carrot, doghouse, goggles, jump rope, lamp, piano

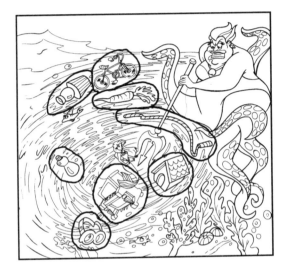

110 Sound Test I

1. June
2. Dune
3. Balloon
4. Cartoon
5. Prune
6. Noon
7. Baboon
8. Raccoon
9. Spoon
10. Maroon
11. Bassoon
12. Lagoon

112 Cracked Up

It's **the lamp**

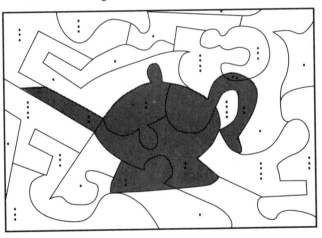

111 Double Vision III

1. Scar's eyebrows are different; 2. The bird is missing in the bottom scene; 3. The giraffe is missing in the bottom scene; 4. The hyenas are standing farther apart in the bottom scene; 5. There's an extra bone in front of the hyenas in the top scene; 6. One of the big rib bones on the ground in front of Scar is missing in the top scene; 7. There's a plant in the lower right corner of the bottom scene; 8. One of the upright bones to the right of the rock is missing in the top scene; 9. The middle hyena's topknot is different; 10. All three hyenas are growling in the bottom scene

169

113 Sneaky Snakes

1. Boa
2. Asp
3. Adder
4. Cobra
5. Viper
6. Garter
7. Python
8. Anaconda
9. Sidewinder
10. Coral Snake
11. Copperhead
12. Rattlesnake

114 Settled Settler

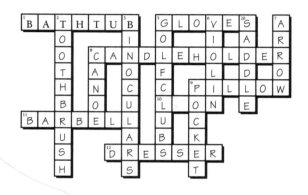

116 See Sounds

Bee, key, knee, pea, ski, tea, three, tree, Z

117 Mirror Image

It's **a scale**

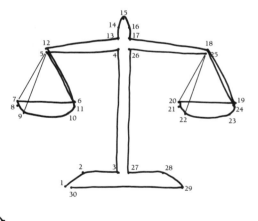

118 Invite Tease

The invitation is for **Anastasia**, who is standing to the far left

119 Rats!

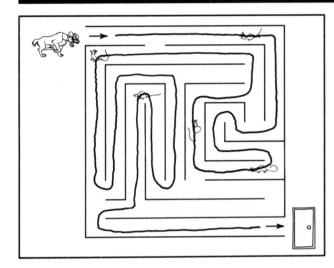

120 Mini-Crosswords II

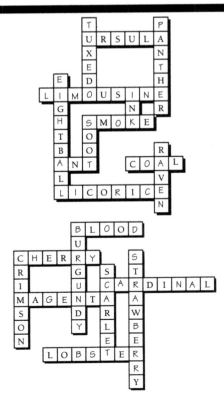

171

ANSWER
PAGE

122 Heads and Feet

There are **five camels** and **thirteen people**

124 Puppy Pairs

125 No Time to Lose

No—she has one hour left

127 Take-Outs III

Box A is taken exactly from the scene

123 Fame and Fortune

1. Yo-yo
2. Revenge
3. Wolf
4. Study
5. Canoe
6. Bulb
7. Ire

Stromboli said, "**Your face will be on everybody's tongue**"

126 Divide and Conquer

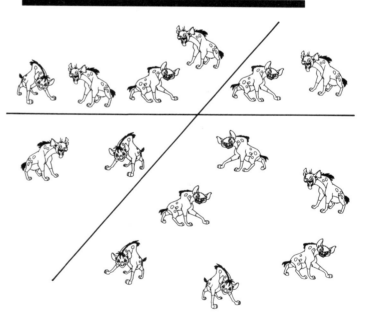

128 Code Names II

1. SYNONYMS FOR UGLY
Hideous
Repulsive
Unsightly
Dreadful
Gruesome
Ghastly
Frightful
Grotesque

2. BIG ANIMALS
Whale
Elephant
Giant Tortoise
Giraffe
Sea Lion
Mammoth
Rhinoceros
Grizzly Bear

3. BIRDS
Parrot
Ostrich
Peacock
Hummingbird
Vulture
Pelican
Woodpecker
Blue Jay

4. BLACK AND WHITE
Dalmatian
Zebra
Checkerboard
Old Movies
Skunk
Piano Keys
One-way Sign
Penguin

130 Home Grown

1. The flower on the right is too large; 2. The door leaning against Alice's left foot is too small; 3. The chair by her left leg is too large; 4. The ladder lying against her right leg is too small; 5. The glove lying on the sidewalk nearby is too large

131 Fowl Play

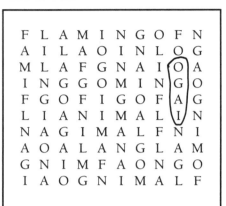

134 Poison Potion

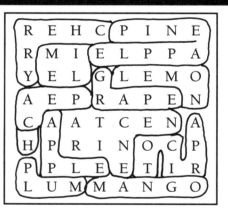

132 Who's Who?

The Stork is really Robin Hood

133 Quick Draw IV

Your drawing should look like this:

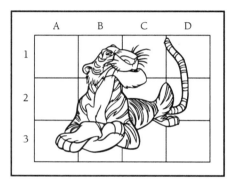

135 How Many Hyenas?

There are **54 hyenas** in Scar's army

136 Sports Rebuses

PUrse + boNneT + a - bone - ears = PUNT
HoUsE - e + paDDLE - Soap = HUDDLE
BeAr + cat + piLLow - pirate - cow = BALL
PAint + SledS -ten - lid = PASS

The sport is **football**

138 Armed with Words

Cane, castle, eels, nets, scale, seal, and tent can be spelled with the letters in tentacles. **Skate** cannot

140 The *I*'s Have It

1. Lightning
2. Lipstick
3. Pinky Ring
4. Windmill
5. Ninth Inning
6. Ski Lift
7. Jiminy
8. Mississippi
9. Bikini

139 Double Vision IV

1. The tree outside the window is missing in the top scene;   2. The window crossbars are different; 3. The left stepsister's feather is turned different ways;   4. Cinderella's necklace is different;   5. Cinderella's left arm is in a different position; 6. The wallpaper pattern is missing in the bottom scene;   7. The right stepsister has a bow on her dress in the bottom scene;   8. The doorknob is missing in the bottom scene;   9. The right stepsister's expression is different; 10. One of the folds in the curtain extends farther in the top scene

141 Next in Line

The bulldog should go next—he's standing, and facing left

142 Undercover Work

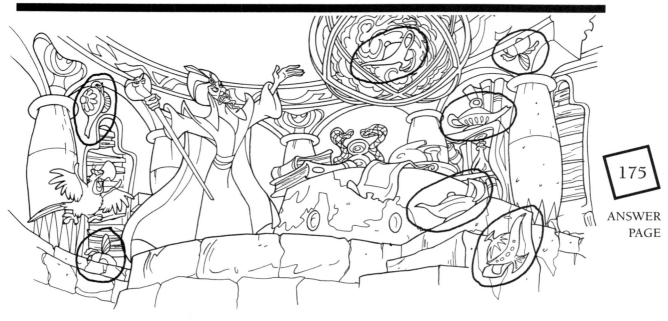

144 Sound Test II

1. Red
2. Sped
3. Fled
4. Bread
5. Sled
6. Tread
7. Read
8. Head
9. Fed
10. Bed

145 Home Run

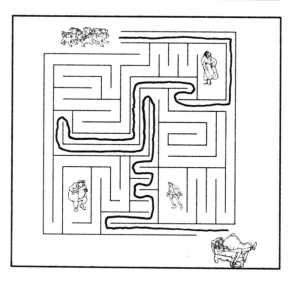

146 Villain Vexation

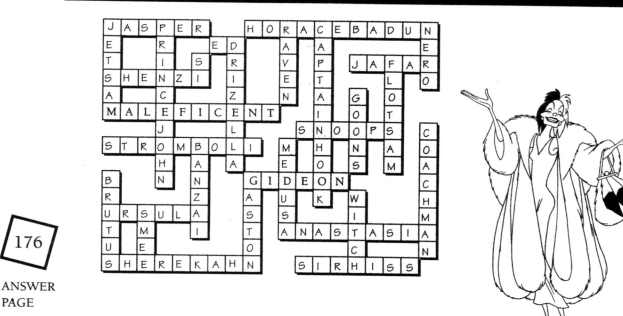